Japanese Pickled Vegetables

129 Homestyle Recipes for Traditional Brined, Vinegared and Fermented Pickles

Machiko Tateno

TUTTLE Publishing

Tokyo | Rutland, Vermont | Singapore

Contents

CHAPTER 1: The Basics

CHAPTER 3: Instant Pickles

Foreword

Unlike Western pickles that are treated as add-ons and condiments, *tsukemono*, preserved or fermented foods, are pickles with a purpose. An essential part of the Japanese meal, they add color, are good for the gut, offer complimentary textures and tastes and provide vitamins and minerals. A traditional Japanese meal consists of rice, soup, three side dishes and pickles to be eaten at the end of the meal to aid digestion. Some Japanese even define a complete meal as rice, soup and pickles.

When I first went to Japan as a young student in 1972, our dormitory's cafeteria always served *takuan* daikon radish pickles at the table, no matter what the main course. Neon yellow, salty and crunchy, I grew to enjoy them almost as much as sour pickles, kraut and green tomatoes, the holy trinity of the New York deli table of my youth.

Some years later, a Japanese friend let me in on her stash of homemade fermenting food. She lifted a hidden floorboard to reveal crocks of miso, *umeboshi* pickled plums and a pungent aromatic bed of *nukadoko* rice-bran mash from which she plucked an eggplant that she sliced to accompany our lunch. Over time I learned how to make a few pickles and came to appreciate that the world of Japanese pickles is a universe of its own. Entire shops and districts in cities are devoted to specialty pickles. From train-station gift shops to department stores, you'll find gorgeously wrapped boxes and porcelains containing fermented regional delicacies made from fruit, vegetables and even seafood.

One of my favorites is *kizami shoga*, the red shards of salty ginger that perfectly accent everything from curry rice to *gyudon* beef bowls, and that I use to decorate the *chirashizushi* scattered sushi I make for parties. Until I found this book, I had always bought my *kizami shoga* in a jar, never imagining I could make it myself. But my interest was piqued when I saw homestyle recipes for what I had come to think of as commercial pickles.

Interest turned to inspiration. There was no stopping me. I turned out a jar of Ginger Pickled in Red Plum Vinegar (see page 37) in 12 hours, there is kimchi (popular in Japan, see page 45) fermenting in a dark corner of my basement, and in my fridge now lives a Rice Bran Pickling Bed (see page 19) to which I routinely add eggplants, carrots, celery and daikon that I slice for a virtuous snack with a glass of wine. The author, Machiko Tateno, told me she doesn't only eat pickles with rice—she often tosses tangy tidbits of pickles with lettuce and tomatoes for a unique and healthful salad. Her book is punctuated with practical ideas for using pickles as an ingredient in unexpected ways. Her serving suggestions include Soft Scrambled Eggs with Sweet and Tart Pickled Ginger (see page 35) and a caraway-studded Sauerkraut Soup with bacon and potatoes (see page 137). Revelatory!

People who preserve bring patience to a project. That's good, as you will need it if you are making pickled plums, or plum wine. But there are plenty of quick and easy recipes in Chapter 3 for those with less forbearance!

Some readers will be unfamiliar with ingredients in some of the recipes. Fortunately the global online pantry is keystrokes away, a blessing for those of us who do not live near Asian markets. But ingredients once considered esoteric like miso and kombu are available now at many well-stocked supermarkets. With Tateno-san as your guide you will soon be expanding your pickle palate.

—Debra Samuels
Author of *My Japanese Table*

Introduction

I grew up in a farming household where tsukemono pickles were a common topic of kitchen conversation. We would speculate whether the cucumber pickle might be ready or wish we had some of Mom's special long-fermented pickles—all we needed with a bowl of rice for a satisfying meal.

A simple definition of pickling is "preserving food with salt." Salt not only keeps food from spoiling, the fermentation that occurs during salting results in greater nutritional value and deeper flavor—what we Japanese call umami. This word, now used around the world, describes a fifth taste: savory— after sweet, sour, salty and bitter. This is what makes Japanese pickles special.

What I love about pickling and preserving is the big tent of flavor possibilities. Each batch I make is slightly different from previous ones. All you need is a vegetable, some salt and a little assistance from microorganisms floating in the air. With time, these elements work together to produce something unique and delicious.

This book will introduce you to the art of Japanese pickling and preserving. I devoted an entire year to developing and photographing this collection of traditional, modern and seasonal recipes. My aim is to give readers easy, practical ways to enrich their dinner tables and their health. I hope I have succeeded!

—Machiko Tateno

Notes from the Author

○ For pickles that require substantial aging or that use seasonal ingredients, such as plums, I have calculated finished amounts of pickles that can be enjoyed over a relatively long period. For instant pickles, amounts are sufficient for making enough pickles to be eaten in a relatively short period. Generally the final yield, after salting and marinating, is approximately half the volume you have started with, but bear in mind that the yields given at the head of each recipe are estimates only, and may vary. When the pickling process is complete you may need to use a smaller container for storage.

○ Weights given for salt and other pickling ingredients are based on the weight of the main recipe ingredient.

○ Preparation time given at the head of each recipe is the time needed to prepare the vegetables before they are left to ferment.

Aging
○ Time periods given for aging are the minimum required for the pickles to be ready for eating. Aging is one of multiple factors affecting flavor. Aging at room temperature should be done in a cool, dark place in a location not exposed to direct sunlight, where the temperature is relatively stable.

Storage
○ Storage refers to the period during which a pickle can be enjoyed at its best flavor and texture. When a pickle is being stored, it is being kept in a container, jar, or bag, soaking in the pickling solution, if one is being used.

Containers and Equipment
○ Storage containers, storage bags, jars, weights and other items necessary for preparation and marinating are listed in each recipe. Containers and jars should be clean, with wide mouths, and bags should be new and not previously used. It is presumed that basic items such as knives, saucepans and mixing bowls are part of standard kitchen equipment and are not included on this list.

Measurements
1 teaspoon = 5 ml
1 tablespoon = 15 ml
1 cup = 250 ml

Pickling Equipment

The types of containers, plastic bags and other utensils you'll need are listed at the head of every recipe.

Containers

The type of container you will use depends on the volume of the vegetable or fruit to be preserved, the aging time and storage place. All containers should have lids, be made of a material that will not react to salt or vinegar, and have a large opening for easy access.

Plastic Pots Plastic pots weigh less than enamel ones which makes them easier to work with. Plastic, though, can retain smells. This can be avoided by lining a plastic pot with a high-quality food-grade plastic bag before using.

Enamel Pots Enamel pots have a base that is made of metal, are coated with an enamel finish and do not react to salt or vinegar. For pickles that are made in large amounts and require a relatively long period to mature, enamel pots are ideal. It is best not to use a metal scouring pad to clean them as these pads can cause scratches, which can lead to rust.

Storage Jars and Airtight Jars

Glass storage jars are great for pickles and preserves that involve a lot of liquid, like young ginger, pearl onions and sauerkraut, as they allow you to visually monitor the fermentation process. Airtight seals also help to control strong smells. Some recipes require pouring hot liquid into the storage container. If you select a storage jar for one of these recipes, make sure the jar is made out of heat-resistant glass.

Enamel Boxes Enameled metal boxes are good options for holding pickles in the refrigerator for maturation or storage. I also use them to hold the fermentation medium for making a Rice Bran Pickling Bed (see page 19) and Okara Pickles (see page 84).

Storage Bags

Pickles can be made in plastic bags. Select ones that are sturdy, resealable and food safe.

Zip Lock Bags For making pickles in small batches that have a short maturation period, and small amounts of salt and vinegar, a zip lock storage bag is a good option. The contents can be simply mixed by massaging the bag.

Marinade Bags with Expandable Bottom Resealable expandable bottom marinade bags work as substitutes for storage bottles.

Poly Bags Non-sealable food-grade poly bags are good for pickles that require very little maturation and for easy removal of water from vegetables before beginning the main pickling process. Choose a good quality bag approximately 8 inches (20 cm) wide and 18 inches (46 cm) tall that will provide ample room for the ingredients.

Sterilizing Storage Containers

To ensure success in your fermenting efforts, sterilize storage containers with white distilled liquor that has an alcohol content of at least 35% (70 proof). Japanese shochu or vodka are good options. Sterilize drop lids and weights that will be in direct contact with the vegetables and fermenting medium. Dampen a paper towel with the liquor and wipe the interior surface to be sterilized. For a container or pot pour a bit of the liquor into the container and tilt to cover the surfaces. Discard the liquor when done.

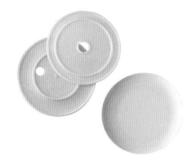

Brining Bags Use brining bags or bucket liner bags to line buckets, pots, cardboard boxes and other containers that you use for storing or aging pickles. This will prevent leakage and contain smells.

Other Equipment

Tea Filter Bags These are available on *Amazon.com*

Digital Scales Pickling requires the use of salt and sugar in proportion to the main ingredient. A good digital kitchen scale is indispensable for accurate measurements. A calculator will also be a handy aid.

Drop Lids A drop lid is used to evenly disperse the downward force of a weight on whatever is being compressed. A drop lid should have a diameter that is only slightly smaller than the inside diameter of the container being used. If you don't have a drop lid, use a plate instead.

Net Cages A net cage stops vegetables from blowing away while drying outdoors.

Weights When aging or storing pickles, weights are essential for efficiently pressing water out of the vegetables. Weights also improve storage by ensuring that pickles remain submerged in the pickling solution. You can buy weights made specifically for pickling, or use bags of flour or bottles of water instead.

Drying Baskets Flat baskets of natural material, like those pictured, are ideal for drying vegetables in the sun. The basket at the bottom of the photo is used for drying plums for umeboshi pickles.

Saucepans Use enamel or stainless steel saucepans to boil pickling solutions with high vinegar content. Avoid aluminum as it is vulnerable to the effects of acid.

Glossary of Ingredients

The list below contains information about Japanese ingredients used in this book, as well as about basic seasonings, such as salt and sugar. Many Japanese ingredients are available from online stockists, Asian markets or well-stocked health food emporia. Read labels carefully, and if possible use brands that are organic with few preservatives. The fresh produce, such as Japanese plums or young ginger, are available seasonally at Asian markets and some farmers' markets. You will need to plan ahead and call your local market to order these items or take your chances when these gems appear. Or you could even try growing your own Japanese herbs and vegetables from seed!

Alum
Alum is a potassium-based powder often used in pickling for retention of color. You can sometimes find it on supermarket shelves alongside the spices. It's an optional touch for a vibrant effect. It's sold by McCormick's. *mccormick.com*

Amazake
This is a thick, fermented, naturally sweet low-alcohol rice wine for drinking, cooking and preserving. You can find it at Asian markets and online, or try making it yourself following the recipe on page 86.

Bonito Flakes
Called *katsuobushi* in Japanese, these are dried flakes of skipjack tuna. You'll find them at Asian markets and online.

Burdock Root
This is a very popular vegetable in Japan, where it is known as *gobo*. You may be able to find it at Asian markets or farmers' markets.

Cucumber
The recipes in this book that call for cucumber use the Japanese variety, which is slender with thin skin. You can substitute Persian, Armenian or mini cucumbers.

Cuttlefish
Called *saki ika* in Japanese, you should be able to find this in your Asian market, either as a whole piece of dried fish or ready-shredded (as a popular snack with drinks).

Dried Cuttlefish
See Cuttlefish.

Dried Sardines
See Sardines.

Eggplants
Japanese eggplants are slender, with thin skin, and are readily available at Japanese grocery stores. You can substitute Chinese eggplant (widely available at Asian markets) or mini Italian and Indian varieties for the recipes in this book. You can also grow your own varieties from scratch with seeds from *kitazawaseed.com*. *See also* Mizu-Nasu.

Kiriboshi Daikon
These are daikon radish strips that have been dried and packaged. Find kiriboshi daikon at your Japanese grocery.

Koji
See Rice Koji.

Kombu Seaweed
Kombu seaweed is sold in dried strips at Asian markets and online. It adds umami and also acts as a thickener. It may be labeled as "dried kelp" or "dashi kombu." The company Emerald Cove carries kombu and is available in many American supermarkets, mostly in stores like Whole Foods, which is a supermarket for organic and healthy food products. Emerald Cove kombu is also available on *Amazon.com*

Light Soy Sauce
See Soy Sauce.

Lotus Root
Lotus root is sold fresh at Asian markets. It is also sometimes sold pre-cooked in pouches.

Mirin
Mirin is a type of sweet rice cooking wine that is a common, everyday ingredient in Japan. You can find it at Japanese groceries. If possible, try to find *hon-mirin*, "real" mirin, which is naturally fermented and made only with water, rice, koji and sometimes salt. Hon-mirin has a natural sweetness and umami enhancing qualities that regular mirin does not, and we recommend it for the recipes in this book if you can find it. It is available in Korean and Japanese groceries and also in natural food emporia such as Eden Foods. Mikawa Organic Mirin is available from *Amazon.com*

Miso
Recipes in this book use miso that has been fermented with rice and matured for 10 months with a salt content of about 12.5%. Miso fermented with barley and soybeans has less salt, so if you use this, add a little extra salt. Take care to read the labels when purchasing miso so as not to choose a brand that contains dashi, a smoky bonito fish stock. You can find many organic miso options in both general and Asian markets.

Mizu-Nasu
This is a small, tender eggplant from Kyoto and the only type of eggplant that can be eaten raw. You may come across it at Asian markets or farmers' markets, or you could try growing your own from seed.

Myoga Ginger Buds
You may find these aromatic buds at Japanese grocery stores. They are also sold by Shopfieldjapan, via *Amazon.com* where they are spelled "mioga."

Okara Soy Pulp
This is the by-product of making tofu. It is available fresh at Japanese and Korean groceries, or from a tofu-maker if you are lucky enough to live near one. This ingredient is also called "tofu lees" or "tofu dregs" in English.

Oriental Pickling Melons
You may find these at Asian markets, or you can grown them from scratch using seeds from *kitazawaseed.com*. Green papaya, chayote Kirby cucumber or regular cucumber all work as substitutes.

Pickled Herring Roe
Called *kazunoko* in Japanese this is a popular New Year's dish in Japan. You can find it in the refrigerated section of your Japanese grocery.

Plums
The umeboshi pickled plum recipes in this book have been made with Japanese varieties such as Nanko, Shirokage and Togoro. Look out for these in late spring at Japanese and Korean groceries or at farmers' markets. The Shiro variety, which is grown in the US can also be used, although it will give a milder taste. Ao-ume (green plums), also grown in the US, can be used to make umeboshi but you will have to let them ripen first. Young apricots can also be used.

Plum Vinegar
The brine produced when making umeboshi pickled plums with red shiso leaves (page 54–55) is red plum vinegar. If making this recipe, you will accumulate a quantity of naturally produced red plum vinegar that can be used in other recipes in this book. Red plum vinegar can also be found commercially prepared, often with the English label "ume plum vinegar." As well as a great pickling medium, it's delicious splashed in salads.

Red Chili Pepper
In this book whole deseeded dried red chilies are used to balance flavors. To turn up the heat, cut the peppers into rings before adding them to the pickling medium.

Rice Bran
There are two types of rice bran used in this book, regular rice bran and roasted rice bran. Regular rice bran is widely available at health food stores. Roasted rice bran (pictured), called *irinuka* in Japanese, is available from Japanese groceries and from online sources such as *Amazon.com*

Rice Koji
Koji, another flavor booster, is steamed rice inoculated with koji fungus, Aspergillus oryzae (lactic acid bacteria), which acts to naturally enhance fermentation and flavor. It is used to make miso, brew soy sauce and sake, and in pickles and alcohol. You can find it sold in dry or fresh form at Asian markets or online. It is also referred to in English as "malted rice."

Rice Vinegar

Rice vinegar is used for most of the vinegared recipes in this book. It has a mild flavor, adds sourness and extends shelf life.

Rock Sugar

Rock sugar is crystallized sugar. It is slightly less sweet than regular sugar and dissolves more slowly. It is readily available in the US at Asian markets, either white or brown, both of which are fine for the recipes in this book. Some brands, such as Chic Crystal White Sugar, are available on *Amazon. com.* You can substitute granulated sugar in recipes that call for rock sugar, with no adjustment of quantities.

Sake

In recipes that call for sake you can use regular drinking sake, such as the Gekkeikan brand, which is widely available in liquor stores. You can also use cooking sake, which you'll find at Asian markets.

Sake Lees

Sake lees, *sake kasu* in Japanese, is the substance left over after making sake. It is flavorful and people long ago discovered it could be used in pickling. Sake lees comes

in dried slabs and as a paste at Japanese groceries. You can also find it in powder form from online sources.

Salt

All recipes in this book call for coarse salt, which has a mild flavor and contains a range of minerals. For initial salting, choose a cheaper salt. For the main pickling process, choose the salt that will give the best flavor. Kosher salt works

well in these recipes. Choose a brand with no additives such as iodine or anti-caking ingredients. These can darken pickles or turn the brine cloudy.

Salted Shrimp and Salted Squid

Find refrigerated in Japanese and Korean groceries. Salted squid is called *ika no shio kara* in Japanese and *ojingeojeot* in Korean; salted shrimp is called *ebi no shio kara* in Japanese and *saeujeot* in Korean.

Sardines

The dried sardines used in some recipes in this book are called *niboshi* in Japanese and you may be able to find them at your Asian market.

Shio Koji

This is a fermented mix of koji rice, salt and water. It comes in paste form and can be found online or in the refrigerated section of Japanese groceries. It is often called "rice malt seasoning" in English.

Shio Kombu

This is a dried, shredded, seasoned kombu seaweed often used as a condiment with rice dishes in Japan. Available at Asian markets and online. It is sometimes labeled in English as "salted kombu" or "salted kelp."

Shiso Leaves and Seeds

Both the leaves of the red and green variety of this plant and the fresh seeds are used in recipes in this book. You may be able to find the leaves at your Asian market and the seeds at farmers' markets. It's easy to grow shiso from scratch. Called "perilla" in English, you may find seeds for planting at your local garden center, or you can order online from *kitazawaseed.com.* You may be able to find ready-to-use preserved red shiso leaves (see photo above) at Japanese groceries.

Soy Sauce

Recipes in this book call for either "soy sauce," which is regular dark Japanese* soy sauce or "light soy sauce."
Regular dark soy sauce has a salt content of 14.5% and is usually fermented with wheat. It adds aroma and umami to food. Light soy sauce is lighter in color and saltier than regular soy sauce. It is used when you don't want to darken the food in the recipe. Do not confuse this with low-sodium soy sauce, which is only lower in salt. We do not recommend low sodium soy sauce due to the additives used in the product. For those with gluten allergies, substitute tamari.

Regular Japanese soy sauce, such as the Kikkoman brand, can be found in most supermarkets. You may need to go to your Japanese grocery for light soy sauce, which is labeled *usukuchi.*

*Japanese soy sauce rather than soy sauce from other countries is recommended for the recipes in this book as the quality varies from country to country.

Shiso Seeds
See Shiso Leaves.

Sugar
Sugar prevents spoilage, extends shelf life and keeps pickles moist. Superfine or castor sugar can be used for the recipes in this book. For a slightly deeper flavor, use light brown sugar or for less sweetness, use granulated sugar. *See also* Rock Sugar.

Umezu
See Plum Vinegar.

Vinegar
See Plum Vinegar *or* Rice Vinegar.

Wasabi Greens
You may be able to find wasabi greens at Asian markets or farmers' markets. The mustard green "Wasabina" is easy to grow with seeds from *kitazawaseed.com*. For a similar spiciness, substitute any kind of mustard greens, although the texture may be different. For a similar texture, try substituting kale or green cabbage.

Yuzu
This Japanese citrus fruit has a distinct sharp flavor. It is periodically available fresh at Korean and Japanese groceries. If you find a fresh yuzu, buy it and remove the zest and juice and freeze for later use. Yuzu juice and yuzu salt are available online. Limes, lemons, grapefruits or a combination of all three can be used as substitutes in recipes.

Online Resources for Japanese Ingredients

USA
Eden Foods Inc. is an organic food producer and purveyor of organic Japanese food products. You can find Eden Foods products in natural food emporia and many large supermarkets in the United States.
edenfoods.com

Japan Super is an authentic Japanese online grocery store.
japansuper.com

Kitazawa Seed Company are the largest grower of Asian vegetable seeds and aromatics in the United States.
kitazawaseed.com

Mikuni Wild Harvest has many fresh Japanese ingredients.
mikuniwildharvest.com

Ohsawa is a Japanese brand of organic ingredients. Available online at Gold Mine Natural Food Company.
shop.goldminenaturalfoods.com

ShopfieldJapan sells through Amazon and Ebay. They have Japanese *rakkyo* onions and myoga ginger buds.

Tokyo Central, Marukai Market
tokyocentral.com

USA and EUROPE
japancentre.com

AUSTRALIA
ichibajunction.com.au

WEBSITES
There are several websites devoted to fermentation and preserving which can provide experienced assistance on pickling and products. We recommend Nami Chen's website and vlog, which covers all aspects of Japanese cuisine, including Japanese pickles. She lives in San Francisco, California and is used to finding ways to work with ingredients at hand.
justonecookbook.com

Chapter 1
The Basics

Many Japanese make their own pickles, devoting time and attention
to the creation of traditional and familiar flavors that will vary slightly
from family to family. Plums, onion, ginger and cabbage are some of
the more popular ingredients found in basic home-pickling in Japan.
And recently kimchi, the fiery Korean condiment, has become a much-
loved addition to the Japanese pickle panorama.

Fermented Rice Bran

Rice bran is the powder from the nutritious outer layer of the rice grain when it is milled. It is the main ingredient for making a fermented mash (called *nukadoko* in Japanese) that serves as a bed for pickling all kinds of vegetables. To make this mash, we use roasted rice bran, called *irinuka* in Japanese, which is stocked at Japanese groceries and is available online. If you can't get hold of already-roasted rice bran, you can toast non-roasted rice bran (available from your local health food store) in a dry skillet over low heat, stirring it with a wooden spoon until it browns.

This traditional Japanese pickling medium produces pickles that range from mild to pungent depending on their time in the mash. Coarse salt, a combination of spices and aromatics like garlic, ginger, dried red chili peppers, dried sardines and dried shiitake mushrooms infuse flavor into the paste and provide umami. Vegetable scraps and trimmings from carrots, daikon radish or cabbage (to name a few) will begin the natural fermentation process. Water and enzymes from the vegetable scraps promote fermentation in the rice bran.

Two weeks after making the mash, it is ready to host vegetables for pickling. Once housed in traditional wooden tubs, today Japanese home cooks use sealed plastic tubs that fit in the refrigerator. The rice bran mash needs to be aerated daily to encourage the growth of good microorganisms. Wash the vegetables and your hands thoroughly and wear plastic gloves when adding or removing vegetables from the mash, so as not to introduce harmful bacteria. Once the pickling bed is established, it can be kept indefinitely with care (not unlike a sourdough starter). There is no limit to the types of vegetable you can pickle in the bed.

Making a Rice Bran Pickling Bed

YIELDS: 2 lbs (1 kg) of pickling medium
PREPARATION TIME: 20 minutes

2 cups (500 ml) water
⅓ cup (70 g) kosher or coarse sea salt (13–14% of the weight of the rice bran)
5 cups (500 g) roasted rice bran (irinuka)
1 dried red chili pepper, deseeded
2 dried sardines (niboshi), head and organs removed, optional
2 small slices fresh ginger
1 piece dried kombu seaweed, 2 in (5 cm) square
1 dried shiitake mushrooms, broken into pieces
½ cup (100 g) assorted vegetable scraps (i.e., carrot and daikon radish peel—keep peel long for easy handling—plus more for replenishing)

CONTAINER ▸ 8 x 8 x 3 in (20 x 20 x 8 cm) storage container with tight-fitting lid
AGING ▸ Up to two weeks (see step 5 below)
STORAGE ▸ Refrigerate, keeps indefinitely

1 Put the water in a large saucepan over medium heat and bring to a boil. Add the salt and stir until it has dissolved. Turn off the heat. Put half the roasted rice bran and half the water in the storage container. Mix well. Add the remainder of the rice bran and water and mix well again.

2 Add the peppers, dried sardines (if using), ginger, kombu and dried mushrooms to the mash and mix thoroughly.

3 Add the vegetable scraps to the container and fold them into the mixture. Smooth the top of the mash. Close the container and keep it in a cool, dark place for 2 to 3 days. Stir the rice bran twice a day if the weather is warm, and once a day if the weather is cool.

4 Remove the vegetable scraps from the rice bran after 2 to 3 days. Add a new batch of vegetable scraps. Place the container in a cool, dark place for 4 to 5 days. Repeat this step 2 to 3 times for up to 2 weeks. This will enhance the fermentation capacity of the mash and make it ready for use. When you add the vegetables to be pickled to the mash, you should store the container in the refrigerator.

HOW TO USE RICE BRAN FOR PICKLING

Generally non-root vegetables should be aged for 1 to 2 days, while root vegetables should be aged for 2 to 3 days. The longer the fermentation, the greater the sourness of the pickle—it's up to you. Different vegetables can occupy the same bed. The following are suggested vegetables, preparation methods and fermentation times.

CARROTS Peel and halve or quarter. Keep in the bed for 2 to 3 days.
CELERY Remove the strings. Keep in the bed for 2 days.
CHERRY TOMATOES Remove stems. Keep in the bed for 1 to 2 days.
CUCUMBER Use the Japanese type. Cut off both ends, and sprinkle with salt. Keep in the bed for 2 days.
EGGPLANTS Make a split down the middle, leaving the stalk end intact. Sprinkle with salt. Keep in the bed for 2 days.
MYOGA JAPANESE GINGER BUDS Leave whole or split. Keep in the bed for 2 days.
DAIKON RADISH Peel and halve or quarter. Keep in the bed for 2 to 3 days.

NOTES AND TIPS

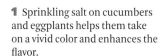

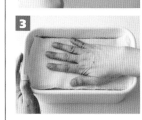

1 Sprinkling salt on cucumbers and eggplants helps them take on a vivid color and enhances the flavor.

2 When the vegetables are ready, remove from the bed, rub as much of the mash from the vegetables as possible and return the mash to the container. Always level off the top of the bed when you have added or removed vegetables. Wipe off any mash that may be stuck to the sides of the container. This helps maintain the bed in the best condition possible.

3 Cover the container and return it to the refrigerator. Water from the vegetables can cause the mash to become waterlogged. Use a paper towel to soak up excess water from the surface of the mash.

FAQ About: Fermented Rice Bran Pickling

Q Is it necessary to mix the fermented rice bran every day?
A Refrigerated rice bran mash ferments slowly so it's not necessary to mix daily. Mixing the mash thoroughly once a week is sufficient. When you remove from the refrigerator to mix, leave the mash at room temperature for a few hours. This will reinvigorate the fermentation bacteria and deepen the flavor in your pickles.

Q Why do my rice bran pickles taste sour and what can I do about it?
A Over-fermentation can result in sour pickles. Add 1 to 2 tablespoons of mustard powder to the mash to reduce the fermentation activity.

Q My pickling bed has a chemical smell. How do I get rid of it?
A The mash should have a natural fermented smell. However, if it is not mixed sufficiently, this can lead to the development of yeast which produces alcohol and gives off a chemical smell. Freeze the mash without the vegetables to reduce the odor.

Q How can I reduce the saltiness of my pickles?
A There are two ways to reduce salt. One is to add some rice bran and water to your mash. The other is to remove the vegetables and only add green or Napa cabbage to the bed. The cabbage will absorb the salt in a few days. The mash may become dry before you resume pickling, so add a bit of water if necessary.

Q What should I do if I won't be using the rice bran mash for a while?
A If you won't be using your mash for weeks or months, remove all the vegetables, level the surface and add a thick layer of coarse salt. You can keep your mash like this at room temperature during the winter. At other times of the year, store it in the refrigerator. When you want to start pickling again, scrape off and dispose of the salt along with the top 1 inch (2.5 cm) layer of bran mash. Alternatively, you can transfer all of the mash to a storage bag and freeze it.

Q Mold has formed on the surface of the mash. What should I do?
A A white growth on the surface of the rice bran is likely to be yeast and you can remove it if you like. If the mold is red, green, or black it must be removed. To do this, discard the mash where the mold is growing, down to a depth of about 1 inch (2.5 cm). Add new rice bran and coarse salt equal to 10% of the weight of the new rice bran. Incorporate thoroughly into the bed.

Q How do I replenish the rice bran mash?
A As you remove pickles from your bed, the amount of mash will decrease. In a separate bowl combine ¾ cup (about 75 g) of roasted rice bran with ½ cup (125 ml) of water and 1 tablespoon of salt and mix well. Add this to the existing bed and mix thoroughly.

These succulent rice-bran pickles are freshly plucked from the rice bran mash. Enjoy pickling seasonal vegetables.

SERVING SUGGESTION
Aged Pickle Salad

If your pickles are over-fermented don't despair. Chop them into small pieces, place in a mesh strainer and briefly rinse with water to remove some of the salt. Put them in a bowl and toss with a dash of soy sauce and sake. It's a great topping for rice. This dish has been around since the start of the 17th century. An old favorite!

SERVING SUGGESTION
Aged Pickle Cheese Spread

This is another tasty use for over-fermented pickles. Rinse the pickles and dice finely. Put in a bowl with cream cheese and coarse ground black pepper to taste. Mix well. This spread is delicious on bread or as a dip for vegetables.

Pickled Condiments

Make your own fantastically flavorful condiments by pickling vegetables and spices. Having these sauces, relishes and dressings on hand will allow you to enjoy seasonal aromas and flavors throughout the year.

Three Kinds of Pickled Peppercorns

Pickle sharply aromatic, numbingly spicy green peppercorns in three ways. Ready for use in only 1 to 2 weeks, these pickled peppercorns are a great complement to a wide variety of dishes.

Peppercorns in Soy Sauce

Salted Peppercorns

Miso-Pickled Peppercorns

SAUTÉED DISHES

Sauté boned pork rib. When the pork fat has dissolved in the pan, add green onions and continue to sauté. Add some Peppercorns in Soy Sauce (page 23) along with some of the pickling liquid.

TIP: Use the soy sauce from Peppercorns in Soy Sauce (page 23) as a dressing for chilled tofu.

SAUCES

When sautéing fish, add Salted Peppercorns (page 23) and butter to the frying pan to make a sauce.

TIP: When a recipe calls for red chili peppers, such as spaghetti peperoncino, try using Salted Peppercorns (page 23) instead.

DRESSINGS

Add sugar and mirin to the miso used to make Miso Pickled Peppercorns (page 23). Use as a dressing for grilled tofu, or as a spread on toast or crackers.

TIP: Mix some of the miso used to make Miso Pickled Peppercorns (page 23) with mayonnaise or butter to make a dip.

PREPARING PEPPERCORNS FOR PICKLING

The recipes on this page are made with fresh green peppercorns on the vine. You can find them at Asian markets or farmer's markets. Follow the steps below to prepare them for pickling.

1 Raw peppercorns can irritate the skin and discolor the nails so you may want to wear plastic gloves. Use a small pair of scissors to cut individual peppercorns from their stems. Make each cut as close to the peppercorn as possible (**photo A**). When finished, rinse the peppercorns in water.

2 Bring a saucepan of water to a boil and add a pinch of salt (**photo B**). Boil the peppercorns for 5–6 minutes, or until you can crush individual peppercorns with your fingers (**photo C**).

3 Transfer the boiled peppercorns to a bowl of cold water and let soak for at least 1 hour (**photo D**). Taste to check; they are ready when you notice a bit of tannin together with some spiciness.

4 Drain the peppercorns and use paper towels to remove excess water (**photo E**).

JAPANESE PEPPERCORNS

You can use regular green peppercorns for the recipes on this page, but if using Japanese peppercorns, note that they come in two types—one that grows in small bunches (right photo) and another that grows in large bunches (left photo). The spiciness of these peppercorns can be reduced by soaking them in water. The longer you soak them, the less spicy they will be.

Miso Pickled Peppercorns

YIELDS: 3 oz (80 g)
PREPARATION TIME: 15 minutes

1 cup (275 g) miso
2 tablespoons mirin
4 oz (115 g) green peppercorns prepared for pickling (see this page)

EQUIPMENT ▸ 1 pint (500 ml) storage container; tea filter bag
AGING ▸ 2 weeks in the refrigerator
STORAGE ▸ Keeps 1 year in the refrigerator

1 Put the miso and mirin in a bowl and mix well. Spread half of this mixture on the bottom of the storage container.

2 Fill the tea filter bag with the peppercorns and place the pack on the top of the layer of the miso-and-mirin mixture in the storage container. Cover the tea filter bag with the remainder of this mixture. Put the storage container into the refrigerator for 2 weeks.

Peppercorns in Soy Sauce

YIELDS: 3 oz (80 g)
PREPARATION TIME: 10 minutes

4 oz (115 g) green peppercorns prepared for pickling (see this page)
½ cup (125 ml) soy sauce

CONTAINER ▸ 1 pint (500 ml) storage jar
AGING ▸ 10 days in the refrigerator
STORAGE ▸ Keeps 1 year in the refrigerator

Make sure the storage jar is very clean. Put in the green peppercorns and soy sauce. Put the jar in the refrigerator for 10 days.

Salted Peppercorns

YIELDS: 3 oz (80 g)
PREPARATION TIME: 10 minutes

4 oz (115 g) green peppercorns prepared for pickling (see this page)
2 teaspoons kosher or coarse sea salt

CONTAINER ▸ 8 oz (225 g) storage jar
AGING ▸ 1 week in the refrigerator
STORAGE ▸ Keeps 1 year in the refrigerator

Make sure the storage jar is very clean. Put in the green peppercorns and the salt. Mix to ensure the salt is evenly distributed. Put the jar in the refrigerator for 1 week.

Yuzu Kosho Green Chili Paste

This tangy and spicy all-purpose condiment, made with Japanese yuzu citrus and green chilies, has long been a favorite in Japan and is becoming popular in the West. If you can't find yuzu, use a combination of equal amounts of lemon, lime and grapefruit zest and juice.

HOW TO USE YUZU KOSHO

• Yuzu Kosho can be used as a condiment for noodles, chicken, sashimi, steak and hotpots.

• Add Yuzu Kosho to dressings for salads and carpaccio.

• Include a pinch of Yuzu Kosho as a secret ingredient in spaghetti sauces.

• Mix Yuzu Kosho with rice vinegar to create a wonderful palate-freshening dipping sauce for gyoza.

• Yuzu Kosho surprisingly pairs well with vanilla ice cream! It also works to bring out the sweetness of desserts that contain cocoa.

YIELDS: 5 tablespoons
PREPARATION TIME: 30 minutes

9–10 green jalapeno peppers
2–3 green yuzu citruses
2 teaspoons kosher or coarse sea salt

EQUIPMENT ▶ Plastic gloves; food processor or mortar and pestle;
½ cup (125 ml) storage jar

AGING ▶ None

STORAGE ▶ Keeps 6 months in the refrigerator; 1 year frozen

FREEZE TO RETAIN COLOR

Yuzu Kosho can be stored in the refrigerator. In the photo above, the jar on the left contains freshly made yuzu kosho. The jar on the right contains yuzu kosho made three days earlier and you can see the color is somewhat faded. To retain the vibrant color of freshly made yuzu kosho, separate your yuzu kosho into small amounts, wrap them in foil, enclose these foil packs in plastic wrap and freeze.

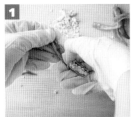

1 Put on a pair of plastic gloves. Cut the stems off the green jalapeno peppers. Halve the peppers and scrape out the seeds. Chop the peppers into small pieces.

2 Peel the green yuzu, taking off a bit of the pith together with the zest. Adding a bit of the pith will add smoothness to the final product.

GREEN YUZU CITRUS

When yuzu mature, they turn yellow. In winter, yuzu are green. The zest of the immature fruit has a cool, fresh aroma, making it ideal for yuzu kosho.

3 Grate or finely chop the zest. You will need 1½ oz (40 g) of yuzu zest.

4 Put the chopped chili peppers and 1 teaspoon of the salt in a food processor and mix briefly.

5 Add the yuzu zest and the remainder of the salt to the food processor. Mix well. If you're using a mortar and pestle, the process is the same. Transfer to the storage jar.

Chopped Salted Lemon

Ready to use in no time, these pickles go with sautéed fish and meat, carpaccio and salads.

YIELDS: 1 cup (100 g)
PREPARATION TIME: 15 minutes

1 organic lemon
Salt for rubbing
1 tablespoon kosher or coarse sea salt (15% of the weight of the lemon)

CONTAINER ▶ 1 cup (250 ml) storage jar
AGING ▶ 1 day in a cool, dark place
STORAGE ▶ Keeps 3 months in the refrigerator

1 Rub the lemon with salt to clean the surface of the peel. Rinse the lemon in water and wipe dry.

2 Cut the lemon into $\frac{1}{4}$ in (5 mm) rounds. Remove the pips. Cut the rounds into $\frac{1}{4}$ in (5 mm) pieces (see photo).

3 Put the lemon and the 1 tablespoon of salt into the storage jar and mix. Leave in a cool, dark place for 1 day.

Pickled Green Chilies

The fish-sauce flavor makes these a great accompaniment to Thai dishes.

YIELDS: 1 cup (100 g)
PREPARATION TIME: 15 minutes

2 green jalapeno peppers
½ cup (125 ml) fish sauce
2 tablespoons mirin

EQUIPMENT ▶ Plastic gloves; 1 cup (250 ml) storage jar
AGING ▶ 1 day in the refrigerator
STORAGE ▶ Keeps 3 months in the refrigerator

1 Wearing plastic gloves, cut off the stems off the peppers. Chop the peppers into small pieces (see photo, below).

2 Put the peppers, fish sauce and mirin in the storage jar and mix. Refrigerate for 1 day.

Miso Marinated Garlic

Over a week of aging, the garlic becomes infused with the salty-sweet umami of miso. The garlic can be used chopped in sautés. Use the miso in sauces, dressings and soups. And if you're seeking the health benefits of garlic, enjoy eating the garlic cloves whole.

YIELDS: 2 cups (250 g)
PREPARATION TIME: 35 minutes

20 garlic cloves
6 tablespoons miso
4 tablespoons mirin

CONTAINER ▶ 1 pint (500 ml) storage jar
AGING ▶ 1 week in the refrigerator
STORAGE ▶ Keeps 6 months in the refrigerator

1 Peel the garlic cloves, place in a sieve and dip them in boiling water for 10 seconds. This will mellow their flavor and promote the pickling process.

2 Put the miso in a mixing bowl, pour in the mirin and mix. Add the garlic cloves and mix.

3 Transfer the contents of the mixing bowl to the storage jar and leave in the refrigerator for 1 week. The Miso Marinated Garlic is ready to use. However, if you plan to eat the garlic cloves whole, let them age for a month first.

Pickled Onions

These sweet and tart Basic Brined Onions are great
as an accompaniment to a main meal or as a snack
with a drink. If you can find the Japanese *rakkyo*
onions pictured here, they are ideal, but pearl onions
also work well (see note, opposite).

Basic Brined Onions (facing page) can be sliced
and served with soy sauce and flakes of smoked
bonito to make a delicious side dish.

Basic Brined Onions

In Japan, this type of pickle is made with an onion called *rakkyo*, which is hard to get in the West, so in this book all recipes for pickled onions call for pearl onions. If you can get hold of rakkyo, remove the root, stem and skin before pickling, and bear in mind that this will reduce their weight by 20–30 percent. This recipe is the basis for the pickled onion recipes on the pages that follow.

YIELDS: approx 2 lbs (1 kg)
PREPARATION TIME: approx 1 hour

1¼ cups (300 ml) water
½ cup (120 g) kosher or coarse sea salt
2 lbs (1 kg) pearl onions, peeled and trimmed

CONTAINER ▸ 1 gallon (4 liter) airtight storage jar
AGING ▸ 2 weeks in a cool, dry place
STORAGE ▸ Keeps up to 1 year in the refrigerator

1 Put the water and salt in a medium saucepan and bring to a boil over medium heat. Remove from the heat and let cool to room temperature. This is the brine.

HOW TO PREPARE THE ONIONS
In an extra large bowl, soak the pearl onions, unpeeled, in plenty of water. Remove the pearl onions from the water and let them dry outside in a shady location, or indoors. Peel before using.

2 Put the onions into the jar and add the cooled brine. Close the jar and keep it in a cool, dark place for about 2 weeks. After 2 weeks, transfer them to the refrigerator and store for up to 1 year.

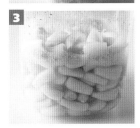

3 As the pearl onions ferment, bubbles will form and the liquid may become cloudy. Neither is a problem. However, it is a good idea to periodically open the jar to release gas.

TO SERVE
To prepare the Basic Brined Onions for eating, take out as many as you need and soak them in plenty of water for 4 to 5 hours to reduce the salt.

Red Pickled Onions

This recipe uses the red plum vinegar that is a by-product of pickling red shiso leaves (see page 55). You can also use readymade red plum vinegar (see Glossary of Ingredients, page 13).

YIELDS: 2 cups (300 g)
PREPARATION TIME: 25 minutes (after soaking)

2 cups (300 g) Basic Brined Onions (see page 29)
½ cup (125 ml) red plum vinegar
½ cup (125 ml) water
5 tablespoons sugar

CONTAINER ▸ 1 quart (1 liter) airtight storage jar
AGING ▸ 2 weeks in the refrigerator
STORAGE ▸ Keeps 6 months in the refrigerator

1 Fill a large bowl with water. Add the Basic Brined Onions and soak for 4 to 5 hours.

2 Set a strainer in the sink and drain the onions. Put them into the jar. Pour in the plum vinegar.

3 Add the water and sugar and seal the jar (**photo A**). Shake the jar to dissolve the sugar. Keep refrigerated for 2 weeks. Occasionally tilt the jar to ensure even development of flavors (**photo B**). After 2 weeks the pickles are ready to eat.

Spicy Pickled Onions

Sichuan peppercorns provide an aromatic spiciness. Finely chopped, these pickles are an excellent topping for chilled tofu.

YIELDS: 2 cups (300 g)
PREPARATION TIME: 25 minutes (after soaking)

2 cups (300 g) Basic Brined Onions (see page 29)
½ cup (125 ml) rice vinegar
5 tablespoons light soy sauce
⅓ cup (50 g) light brown sugar
1 dried red chili pepper, deseeded
1 teaspoon Sichuan peppercorns

CONTAINER ▸ 1 quart (1 liter) airtight storage jar
AGING ▸ 1 week in the refrigerator
STORAGE ▸ Keeps 6 months in the refrigerator

1 Fill a large bowl with water. Add the Basic Brined Onions and soak for 4 to 5 hours.

2 Put the vinegar, soy sauce and brown sugar in a saucepan and bring to a boil over medium heat. Remove the pan from the stove and cool to room temperature.

3 Set a strainer in the sink and drain the onions. Put them into the jar. Put the chili pepper and Sichuan peppercorns on top of the onions. Pour in the cooled liquid and seal the jar. Refrigerate for 1 week. Occasionally tilt the jar to ensure even development of flavors. After a week the pickles are ready to eat.

Honey Ginger Pickled Onions

Apple cider vinegar and honey add a fresh, vibrant taste. Ginger is a perfect match for pickled onions.

YIELDS: 2 cups (300 g)
PREPARATION TIME: 20 minutes (after soaking)

2 cups (300 g) Basic Brined Onions (see page 29)
1 large knob ginger, about 2 oz (50 g), peeled and julienned
½ cup (125 ml) apple cider vinegar
3 tablespoons honey
2 tablespoons sugar

CONTAINER ▸ 1 quart (1 liter) airtight storage jar
AGING ▸ 1 week in the refrigerator
STORAGE ▸ Keeps 6 months in the refrigerator

1 Fill a large bowl with water. Add the Basic Brined Onions and soak for 4 to 5 hours.

2 Put the apple cider vinegar, honey and sugar in a small bowl (**photo A**). Mix until combined.

3 Set a strainer in the sink and drain the onions. Put them into the jar. Put the cut ginger on top of the onions. Add the vinegar mixture (**photo B**). Keep the jar in the refrigerator for about 2 weeks. Occasionally tilt the jar to ensure even development of flavors. After 2 weeks the pickles are ready to eat.

Sweet & Sour Pickled Onions

The addition of mirin and light brown sugar to Basic Brined Onions results in a rich flavor after only 2 weeks.

YIELDS: 2 cups (300 g)
PREPARATION TIME: 15 minutes (after soaking)

2 cups (300 g) Basic Brined Onions (see page 29)
½ cup (125 ml) soy sauce
½ cup (125 ml) mirin
4 tablespoons sake
1 tablespoon light brown sugar
1 piece dried kombu seaweed, 2 in (5 cm) square
1 dried red chili pepper, deseeded

CONTAINER ▸ 1 quart (1 liter) airtight storage jar
AGING ▸ 2 weeks in the refrigerator
STORAGE ▸ Keeps 6 months in the refrigerator

1 Fill a large bowl with water. Add the Basic Brined Onions and soak for 4 to 5 hours (**photo A**).

2 Put the soy sauce, mirin, sake, sugar and kombu in a saucepan and bring to a boil over medium heat. Remove from the heat and cool to room temperature.

3 Set a strainer in the sink and drain the onions. Put them into the jar. Add the cooled liquid from the pan (**photo B**). Keep the jar in the refrigerator for 2 weeks. Occasionally tilt the jar to ensure even development of flavors. After 2 weeks the onions are ready to eat.

Pickled Onions in Sweet Vinegar

In this classic pickling method, Basic Brined Onions (see page 29) are marinated in sweetened vinegar.

YIELDS: 1 lb (450 g)
PREPARATION TIME: 25 minutes

1 lb (450 g) Basic Brined Onions (see page 29)
¾ cup (180 ml) rice vinegar
½ cup (100 g) sugar
1 dried red chili pepper, deseeded

CONTAINER ▸ 1 quart (1 liter) airtight storage jar
AGING ▸ 2–3 weeks in the refrigerator
STORAGE ▸ Keeps 6 months in the refrigerator

1 Fill a large bowl with water. Add the Basic Brined Onions and soak for 4–5 hours

2 Put the vinegar and sugar in a medium saucepan. Bring to a boil over medium heat. Remove from heat.

3 Drain the onions in a colander. Transfer to the jar, pour in the sweetened vinegar, add the red chili pepper and seal the jar. Put in a dark place for 2–3 weeks.

SERVING SUGGESTION
Pickled Onion Tartar Sauce

Make a delicious tartar sauce by mixing chopped Pickled Onions in Sweet Vinegar (above), hard-boiled eggs, mustard, salt and mayonnaise.

Quick Pickled Onions

In this easy recipe there is no initial brining. Fresh pearl onions are boiled and put directly into the marinating mixture. Boiling reduces the water content of the onions and speeds the fermentation process so they are ready to eat in only a month.

YIELDS: 1 lb (450 g)
PREPARATION TIME: 1 hour

1 lb (450 g) pearl onions, trimmed (see note, page 29)
¾ cup (180 ml) rice vinegar
½ cup (100 g) sugar
½ cup (125 ml) water
1½ tablespoons kosher or coarse sea salt
1 dried red chili pepper, deseeded

CONTAINER ▸ 1 quart (1 liter) airtight jar
AGING ▸ 1 month in a cool, dry place
STORAGE ▸ Keeps in a cool, dark place for 1 year

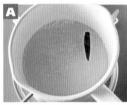

1 Put the pearl onions in plenty of water in a large bowl and wash off any dirt. Drain in a colander.

2 To make the marinating mixture, put all the other ingredients in a medium saucepan. On medium heat bring to a boil. Remove from heat.

3 Fill a second large saucepan ¾ full with water. On medium heat bring to a boil. Add the onions and boil for 10 seconds. Place a colander in the sink and drain the onions.

4 Transfer the onions to the jar and pour in the marinating mixture made in step 2. Seal the jar and keep in a cool, dark place for 1 month. Store in a cool, dark place for up to a year. In warm weather transfer to the refrigerator.

Ginger Pickles

Many Japanese pickles recipes make use of
young ginger. You may be able to find young
succulent ginger in the early summer at
Asian markets. There is barely any skin, the
tips have a red tinge and the taste is mild.
If you do not have access to young ginger
use ordinary mature ginger for these recipes.
Make sure the ginger is fresh and smooth
with no dry or wrinkled areas. The recipes in
this section contain notes for readers working
with mature ginger.

Sweet and Tart Pickled Ginger

The action of the vinegar on the red fibers of young ginger will cause the contents of the jar to take on a slight blush of pink, like the thin pickled slices of *gari* ginger that are served with sushi.

YIELDS: 1 lb (450 g)
PREPARATION TIME: 1 hour

1 lb (450 g) young ginger (or mature ginger)
Water, for soaking plus more for boiling
3 teaspoons kosher or coarse sea salt
¾ cup (180 ml) rice vinegar
¾ cup (180 ml) water
½ cup (100 g) sugar

CONTAINER ▶ 1 quart 1 liter) airtight storage jar
AGING ▶ 12 hours in a cool, dark place
STORAGE ▶ Keeps 6 months in the refrigerator

YOUNG GINGER

Young ginger is sent to market immediately after harvesting, at the start of summer. You may be able to find it at Asian markets. Look for young ginger that is slender with the red portions vibrantly colored. Mature ginger, available throughout the year, can also be used for pickles although the flavor is stronger and the texture is more fibrous.

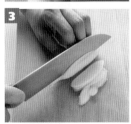

5 While the ginger slices are still hot, sprinkle on 2 teaspoons of the salt. Once the ginger slices have cooled enough to handle, knead for about 1 minute. Squeeze out as much liquid as you can and put the ginger slices into the jar.

6 Put the vinegar, water, sugar and remaining salt into a saucepan and bring to a boil over medium heat. Remove from the heat. Pour the sweetened vinegar into the jar. Seal the jar and keep in a cool, dark place for 12 hours.

1 Separate the ginger into individual knobs for easy slicing. If using young ginger, trim off the top of the stem, leaving about ¼ in (5 mm) of the red portion.

2 Use a spoon to gently scrape off any brown places on the new ginger. Red areas are not a problem. If using mature ginger use a spoon or vegetable peeler to scrape off the dried skin.

3 With a sharp knife or vegetable peeler, thinly slice the ginger lengthwise. Fill a large bowl with water and soak the slices for about 10 minutes.

SERVING SUGGESTION
Soft Scrambled Eggs with Sweet and Tart Pickled Ginger

Heat sesame oil in a skillet and pour in beaten eggs seasoned to taste. Add julienned Sweet and Tart Pickled Ginger and cook until the eggs are soft and creamy.

4 Bring a saucepan of water to a boil over medium heat. Add the ginger slices. When the pan comes back to a boil, wait 1 minute then remove from the heat. Drain the ginger in a colander. If using mature ginger, boil for 3 minutes to reduce the spiciness.

Honey Pickled Ginger

This quick recipe for young ginger preserved in honey is wonderful on toast, with yogurt and as a beverage mixed with soda water or hot water.

YIELDS: ⅔ cup (300 g)
PREPARATION TIME: 10 minutes

4 oz (115 g) young ginger (or mature ginger)
⅔ cup (200 g) honey

CONTAINER ▸ 1 pint (500 ml) airtight storage jar
AGING ▸ 3 days in a cool, dark place
STORAGE ▸ Keeps 6 months in the refrigerator

1 Prepare the ginger as in Sweet and Tart Pickled Ginger (see page 35), steps 1 and 2. Slice thinly, lengthwise.

2 Put the ginger slices into the jar, pour in the honey, close the jar and set aside for 3 days.

Honey mixed with ginger becomes something tasty in its own right, in just 3 days!

Serve in hot water with yuzu citrus zest. Meyer or regular lemon zest can also be used. This is a great drink if you have a cold.

Ginger Pickled in Sweet Kombu Vinegar

This vinegar-based pickle gets a flavor boost from the salt and umami of kelp tea powder. It's perfect as a palate cleanser between dinner courses, as a garnish and in salads.

YIELDS: 12 oz (350 g)
PREPARATION TIME: 45 minutes

12 oz (350 g) young ginger (or mature ginger)
2 teaspoons kosher or coarse sea salt
¾ cup (180 ml) rice vinegar
½ cup (125 ml) water
1 piece dried kombu seaweed, 2 in (5 cm) square
1 tablespoon kelp tea powder
3 tablespoons light brown sugar

CONTAINER ▸ 1 quart (1 liter) heat-resistant storage jar
AGING ▸ 12 hours in a cool, dark place
STORAGE ▸ Keeps 6 months in the refrigerator.

1 Prepare the ginger as in Sweet and Tart Pickled Ginger (see page 35), steps 1 and 2. Julienne the ginger. Soak in a bowl of water for 10 minutes.

2 Bring half a medium saucepan of water to boil over medium heat. Add the ginger and bring the water back to a boil for 2 minutes. Drain the ginger in a colander. Sprinkle on the salt while hot. When cool, gently knead the ginger and squeeze out the excess water. Put the ginger into the jar.

3 Put all the other ingredients in a small saucepan and bring to a boil over medium heat (**photo A**). Remove from the heat and stir until the sugar has melted. While hot, pour the contents of the pan over the ginger (**photo B**). Close the jar and let rest for 12 hours. Remove the kombu before storing.

The ginger softens as it steeps. The liquid will rise to just cover the ginger.

Ginger Pickled in Red Plum Vinegar

This red ginger, called *beni shoga* in Japanese, is often served with curry or beef bowls in Japan. The color of these all-natural homemade pickles won't be as bright as that of commercial products, but you'll find them just as tasty.

YIELDS: 8 oz (225 g)
PREPARATION TIME: 35 minutes

8 oz (225 g) young ginger (or mature ginger)
1 tablespoon kosher or coarse sea salt
1 teaspoon granulated sugar
½ cup (125 ml) red plum vinegar

EQUIPMENT ▸ 1 pint (500 ml) airtight storage container; plastic wrap; small mixing bowl to use as a weight
AGING ▸ 12 hours to 2 weeks in a cool, dark place
STORAGE ▸ Keeps 6 months in the refrigerator

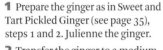

1 Prepare the ginger as in Sweet and Tart Pickled Ginger (see page 35), steps 1 and 2. Julienne the ginger.

2 Transfer the ginger to a medium mixing bowl and add the salt. Place a sheet of plastic wrap directly on top of the ginger. The sheet should be big enough to run up the inside of the bowl and over the sides. Fill a second mixing bowl with water and place it on top of the wrap (**photo A**). Set the bowls aside for 2 hours.

3 Remove the water-filled bowl and the wrap. Squeeze the excess water out of the ginger and transfer the ginger to the storage container. Add the sugar and red plum vinegar (**photo B**). Close the container and put in a cool, dark place for 12 hours.

SERVING SUGGESTION
Red Ginger Skewers

This recipe uses whole red ginger knobs (see bottom left), thinly sliced and threaded onto bamboo skewers. Dip the skewered ginger in a batter of flour, egg and water. Coat with breadcrumbs and fry.

SERVING SUGGESTION
Deep-fried Fish Cake with Pickled Ginger

Chikuwa is tube-shaped Japanese fish cake. Cut into bite-size pieces then halve. Fill the halves with julienned red ginger. Dip in a batter of flour, water and aonori seaweed flakes and fry. You'll find chikuwa and aonori at Japanese groceries.

If using whole knobs of ginger, age for about 2 weeks.

If using julienned ginger, age for 12 hours.

Sweet Soy Marinated Ginger

This makes a wonderful topping for hard-boiled eggs or tofu.

YIELDS: 1 cup (200 g)
PREPARATION TIME: 45 minutes

8 oz (225 g) young ginger (or mature ginger)
½ cup (125 ml) soy sauce
4 tablespoons mirin
1 tablespoon light brown sugar
2 tablespoons rice vinegar
1 teaspoon sesame oil

CONTAINER ▸ 1 pint (500 ml) airtight storage jar
AGING ▸ 2 days in a cool, dark place
STORAGE ▸ Keeps 6 months in the refrigerator

1 Prepare the ginger as in Sweet and Tart Pickled Ginger (page 35), steps 1 and 2. Cut the ginger into thin slices and then mince.

2 Put the soy sauce, mirin, sugar and vinegar in a saucepan and bring to a boil over medium heat. Remove from the heat and cool to room temperature.

3 Transfer the minced ginger to the jar and pour in the sauce (**photo A**).

4 Add the sesame oil to the jar (**photo B**). Close the jar and keep in a cool, dark place for 2 days, after which it is ready to eat.

Miso Pickled Ginger

One day of brining and two weeks of fermenting perfectly blend the spiciness of ginger and the sweetness of miso.

YIELDS: 12 oz (350 g)
PREPARATION TIME: 40 minutes

12 oz (350 g) young ginger (or mature ginger)
2 tablespoons kosher or coarse sea salt) (10% of the weight of the ginger)
1 cup (275 g) miso
1 cup (180 g) light brown sugar

EQUIPMENT ▸ 1 gallon (4 liter) resealable storage bag; 2 metal trays; weights totaling about 1lb (450 g)
AGING ▸ 2 weeks in the refrigerator
STORAGE ▸ Keeps 6 months in the refrigerator

1 Prepare the ginger as in Sweet and Tart Pickled Ginger (page 35), steps 1 and 2. Separate the ginger into knobs. Put the knobs into the bag, add the salt and seal the bag. Massage the bag to rub the salt into the ginger, working from the top.

2 Place the bag containing the ginger on a metal tray. Place a second tray on top of the ginger and place the weight on the top tray. Put the trays into the refrigerator for 1 day.

3 Drain any water that has accumulated around the salted ginger. In a bowl, mix together the miso and sugar. Put into the bag with the ginger. Seal the bag and work the miso around the ginger so it is evenly distributed. Flatten the bag and store in the refrigerator. The pickles will be ready in 2 weeks.

Spiced Ginger Syrup

Use this delicious syrup to make your own ginger ale or ginger tea. The combination of ginger and lemon juice gives the syrup a blush-pink hue. Red chili pepper adds a hint of spice.

YIELDS: 2 cups (500 ml)
PREPARATION TIME: 45 minutes

1 lb (450 g) young ginger (or mature ginger)
1 cup (200 g) granulated sugar
⅓ cup (100 g) honey
Pinch of kosher or coarse sea salt
1 cinnamon stick
10 cloves
2 dried red chili peppers, deseeded
½ cup (125 ml) lemon juice

EQUIPMENT ▸ Storage jar
AGING ▸ None
STORAGE ▸ Keeps 3 months in the refrigerator

1 Grate the ginger with the skin on. (If using mature ginger, peel first.)

2 Put the grated ginger, sugar, honey, salt, cinnamon stick, cloves and red chili peppers in a medium saucepan. Mix well and let stand for 30 minutes. Over medium heat, bring the pan to a boil, reduce heat to low and simmer for 10 minutes.

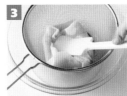

3 Place a sieve on top of a mixing bowl. Line the sieve with a paper towel. Pour in the ginger mixture. After the liquid has drained, fold the edges of the paper towel around the ginger and spices and press with a rubber spatula to remove as much liquid as possible.

4 Add the lemon juice to the bowl and mix. The liquid will gradually turn slightly pink. This is your ginger syrup, which is ready to use. Transfer it to a jar and refrigerate. To make a cold drink, fill a cup a quarter full of syrup and top off with soda water or plain water. Alternatively add hot water for a soothing tea.

Cabbage Pickles

The pickles in this section use the type of cabbage known as *hakusai* in Japanese, or Chinese or Napa cabbage in English. In this section, you'll learn the traditional Japanese way of pickling cabbage, from drying through initial salting to the main pickling process. The liquid extracted from the cabbage during the salting process allows for the growth of lactic acid bacteria, which boosts umami. This is the secret behind the amazing flavor of these delicious pickles.

Pickled Napa Cabbage

On the following pages you'll learn how to make traditional salted and fermented, aged cabbage pickles as well as a quick version for when you just can't wait.

YIELDS: 1½ lbs (700 g)
PREPARATION TIME: 35 minutes

1 head Napa cabbage, about 3 lbs (1.4 kg)
Kosher or coarse sea salt for initial salting
   (2.5% of the weight of the dried Napa cabbage)
Kosher or coarse sea salt for the main pickling process
   (0.5% of the weight of the salted Napa cabbage)
1 piece dried kombu seaweed, 2 in x 4 in (5 cm x 10 cm)
1 dried red chili pepper, deseeded

EQUIPMENT ▶ 2 gallon (7.5 liter) resealable plastic bag; cardboard box, weights totaling 6 lbs (2.7 kg); 5 quart (5 liter) enameled metal container with lid; drop lid (or use a flat plate as a lid)
AGING ▶ 1 day in a cool, dark place for initial salting; 5 days in a cool, dark place for the main pickling process
STORAGE ▶ Keeps 2 weeks (in brine) in a cool, dark place in winter, or 5 days in the refrigerator (removed from brine)

INITIAL SALTING PROCESS

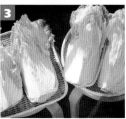

1 With a knife make a cut that goes through the lower core of the cabbage, but not through the upper leaves. With your hands pull the cabbage apart into halves. This keeps the leaves intact.

2 Repeat this procedure to split each half, so that the cabbage is now quartered.

3 Put the cabbage quarters on a flat surface, with the cut surfaces facing up. Dry the cabbage in the sun for about 4 hours. If it's cloudy, dry for an entire day. You can also do the drying indoors.

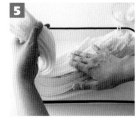

4 Weigh the cabbage quarters and calculate 2.5% of that figure in salt.

5 Rinse the quarters and shake out excess water. Lay on a baking sheet, leaf side up. Use ⅔ of the salt to evenly sprinkle between each leaf of the cabbage quarters. Spread the remaining salt evenly over the cabbage.

6 Put the cabbage in the plastic bag with the cut surfaces facing up and the quarters alternating top and bottom. Place the bag in the cardboard box. Press the air out of the bag and seal.

7 Place weights equal to about twice the weight of the cabbage on top of the plastic bag. Set the box aside in a cool, dark place for one day. After 24 hours, the cabbage will lose water and soften (see picture, below).

MAIN PICKLING PROCESS

8 Remove the cabbage quarters from the bag and squeeze out the water. Rinse and dry the bag and set aside to use again later.

9 Weigh the cabbage and calculate 0.5% of that figure in salt. This is where you may want to use a higher quality salt.

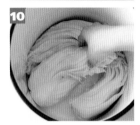

10 Spread half of the measured salt on the bottom of the enameled container and then put in the cabbage. Pack to exclude as much air as possible. Make the top of the cabbage as level as possible.

11 Spread the remaining salt on top of the cabbage. Add the kombu and red chili peppers.

12 Place a drop lid or plate on top of the cabbage. Into the clean plastic bag from step 8, put a weight equal to the weight of the cabbage and place it on top of the drop lid or plate.

13 Put the lid on the container and leave in a cool, dark place. The cabbage will be ready to eat in about five days. As long as it's soaking in the brine produced by the pickling process, it will keep for 2 weeks. If you remove it from the brine, it will keep for 5 days in the refrigerator.

ARE YOUR CABBAGE PICKLES TOO SOUR?
As the lactic acid fermentation continues, it will produce more umami and the pickles will become increasingly sour. Heat reduces the sourness; so try adding the pickles to a soup or hotpot.

ADDITIONAL FLAVORS

Adding small amounts of other flavorful ingredients gives a twist to Pickled Napa Cabbage. Starting from the middle and moving clockwise, the photo shows dried persimmon peel (for sweetness), apple peel (for aroma), roasted soybeans (for umami), garlic and ginger (for a touch of spice) and yuzu or lemon zest (for extra tang).

Quick Napa Cabbage Pickles

This is a great way to make a quick cabbage pickle. The trick is to massage the cabbage, which softens it and makes it ready to eat in minutes.

YIELDS: 12 oz (350 g)
PREPARATION TIME: 30 minutes

½ head Napa cabbage, about 1½ lbs (700 g)
1½ tablespoons kosher or coarse sea salt (3% of the weight of the Napa cabbage)
1 piece dried kombu seaweed, 2 in (5 cm) square
1 dried red chili pepper, deseeded

CONTAINER ▶ 1 gallon (4 liter) storage bag
AGING ▶ 20 minutes at room temperature
STORAGE ▶ Keeps 1 week in the refrigerator

1 Cut the cabbage into 2-in (5 cm) squares and place in the bag. Add the salt.

2 With a little air in the bag, hold it closed and shake to ensure all of the cabbage is evenly salted.

3 Add the kombu and red chili pepper. Squeeze the air out of the bag, seal it and massage the cabbage through the bag to help the cabbage absorb the salt. Set the bag aside for about 20 minutes.

After massaging the cabbage through the bag and letting it rest for 20 minutes, the cabbage softens and its bulk reduces by half.

Serve with a sprinkle of Japanese shichimi 7-spice powder, and a dash of soy sauce.

SERVING SUGGESTION
Pickled Cabbage Sushi Roll

Make a dressing of 3 parts rice vinegar and 1 part sugar and mix with cooked short grain white rice to make sushi rice. Cover a sushi-rolling mat with plastic wrap. Place pickled cabbage leaves on the wrap so they partially overlap. Spread sushi rice on top of the leaves. Add a layer of finely chopped raw tuna and some julienned Crunchy Daikon Pickles (see page 74). Roll, cut and serve. Sprinkle with shichimi 7-spice powder if you like.

Kimchi

Kimchi is the famously funky fermented cabbage dish from Korea. Korean food is very popular in Japan and so is kimchi. The flavor of kimchi is determined by its combination of aromatics, seasonings and the fermentation process. Master the seasonings and you can make kimchi with any vegetable. This recipe uses traditional ingredients such as salted squid and salted shrimp and dried sardines, all available at Korean and Japanese groceries. The salted shrimp and salted squid are in the refrigerator section. If you are unable to source the shrimp and squid or do not wish to use them, no problem. The kimchi will have a lighter flavor but still be delicious! I've included a great recipe for Vegan Kimchi on page 47

Traditional Napa Cabbage Kimchi

YIELDS: about 1½ lbs (700 g)

PREPARATION TIME: 2 hours plus drying time and 1 day for initial salting

1 head Napa cabbage, about 3 lbs (1.4 kg)
3 tablespoons kosher or coarse sea salt for initial salting (about 2.5% of the weight of the dried Napa cabbage)
1 piece daikon radish, about 8 oz (225 g), peeled and julienned
1 carrot, peeled and julienned
⅓ teaspoon kosher or coarse sea salt
Handful chives, about 1½ oz (40 g), cut into ¼ in (5 mm) pieces
1 tablespoon pine nuts

Kimchi Seasoning Paste (makes approx 1 cup [300 g])

1 cup (30 g) dried sardines (niboshi)
½ cup (125 ml) water to make the stock
2 tablespoons rice flour plus ½ cup (125 ml) water
Half an apple or Asian pear, peeled, deseeded and coarsely chopped
5 large garlic cloves, peeled and trimmed
Knob of fresh ginger, about 1½ oz (40 g) peeled and coarsely chopped
3 tablespoons salted squid, optional
3 tablespoons salted shrimp, optional
2½ tablespoons finely ground Korean red chili pepper powder
2½ tablespoons coarse Korean red chili pepper powder
1 tablespoon sugar
1½ tablespoons fish sauce

EQUIPMENT ▸ Flat basket for drying; plastic gloves; 2 gallon (7.5 liter) resealable plastic bag; heavy cardboard box; weights totaling 7 lbs (3 kg); 5 quart (5 liter) nonreactive container with lid; large plastic bag to fit inside the container

AGING ▸ 1 day in a cool, dark place for initial salting; 4 to 14 days for the main pickling process

STORAGE ▸ Keeps 2 weeks in the refrigerator; 2 months frozen

DRYING THE CABBAGE

1 With a knife make a cut that goes through the lower core of the cabbage, but not through the upper half of the leaves. Use your hands to pull the cabbage into halves. Repeat this procedure to split both of the halves, so that you have 4 quarters.

2 Lay the cabbage quarters on a flat basket, cut surfaces facing up. Let the cabbage dry in the sun or by sunny window for about 4 hours. If cloudy, dry for an entire day. You can also do the drying indoors.

SALTING THE CABBAGE

3 Weigh the dried cabbage quarters and calculate 2.5% of that figure in salt. Rinse the cabbage and shake off the excess water. Use ⅔ of the salt to evenly sprinkle between each of the leaves of the cabbage quarters. Spread the rest of the salt evenly over the outsides of the cabbage.

4 Place the cabbage into the plastic bag with cut surfaces facing up and the quarters alternating top and bottom. Press the air out of the bag and seal. Place the bag in the cardboard box. Place weights equal to about twice the weight of the cabbage on top. Set the box aside in a cool, dark place for one day.

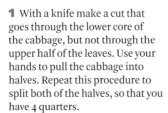

5 Put the julienned daikon and carrot in a bowl. Sprinkle with the ⅓ teaspoon salt and set aside for about 10 minutes. With your hands, squeeze out the liquid.

PREPARING THE KIMCHI SEASONING PASTE

6 To make the stock, remove the heads and organs from the sardines. Put the sardines and the ½ cup of water in a medium saucepan. On high heat bring to full boil. Reduce the heat to low and simmer for 3 minutes. Set a strainer over a bowl and pour the mixture into the strainer. Reserve the liquid and discard the fish.

7 In a separate saucepan mix the rice flour and the ½ cup of water. Use a spatula to break up any lumps. Turn on the heat to medium and continuously stir the mixture. Allow to simmer until the mixture thickens, about 1 minute. Remove from heat.

8 To make the seasoning paste put the apple, garlic, ginger, salted squid and salted shrimp if using, into a food processor and process into a paste. Transfer the paste to a mixing bowl, add both chili powders and sugar and mix well.

9 Add the rice flour mixture from step 7 and mix to incorporate thoroughly.

10 Add the stock made in step 6 and the 3 tablespoons of fish sauce. Mix thoroughly.

11 Add the daikon, carrots and chives and mix well. Finally, mix in the pine nuts.

STORING THE KIMCHI SEASONING PASTE

The seasoning paste can be used to make other kinds of kimchi such as Honey Daikon Kimchi and Mustard Spinach Kimchi (see both recipes on page 48). Store in an airtight jar for 1 month refrigerated, or 6 months frozen.

12 Remove the cabbage from the bag and squeeze out the water. Place on a baking sheet or in a deep dish. Put on a pair of plastic gloves. Working with one cabbage quarter at a time, spread a quarter of the kimchi paste mixture between each leaf of the cabbage, except for the outermost leaf.

13 Fold each of the cabbage quarters in half, so that the outermost leaf remains on the outside. Wrap the outermost leaf around the folded cabbage quarter to secure it.

14 Open the large plastic bag and place it inside your container. Place the cabbage quarters in the bag and pack together tightly. Remove the air from the bag and seal it.

15 Cover the container and set it aside in a cold place for about one week if you are making kimchi in the winter. If you are making it in the summer, set it aside for 1 day in a cool, dark place and then refrigerate for 5 days. Look inside the container periodically to check if the bag has puffed up from naturally released gases during the fermentation process. If it has, open the bag slightly and let the air out. The kimchi should be ready to eat in 4 to 5 days. For a stronger tasting, more fermented kimchi you can age for an additional 1 to 2 weeks. When the kimchi reaches your desired taste, transfer it to the refrigerator.

STORAGE TIPS
Kimchi is pungent, so to prevent your whole refrigerator from smelling like kimchi, store your kimchi in a resealable plastic bag or airtight metal container.

AGED KIMCHI
Kimchi continues to ferment once it's made and this can cause it to become too sour for some. Don't worry! It makes a great ingredient in hotpots or stir-fries. Heating it takes the edge off the sourness and enhances the flavor.

WHEN TO CUT KIMCHI
For the best flavor and texture cut the kimchi just before serving.

SALTED SHRIMP AND SALTED SQUID
These can be found in the refrigerated section of Japanese and Korean groceries. Salted squid (top) is called *ika no shio kara* in Japanese and *ojingeojeot* in Korean; salted shrimp (bottom) is called *ebi no shio kara* in Japanese and *saeujeot* in Korean.

Vegan Kimchi

This quick and easy vegan version of kimchi packs a punch and crunch.

YIELDS: 12 oz (350 g)
PREPARATION TIME: 30 minutes

5 large garlic cloves, peeled and trimmed
Small knob ginger
⅓ Napa cabbage, about 1 lb (450 g), coarsely chopped
Small piece daikon radish, about 3 oz (80 g) peeled and julienned
½ cup (50 g) thinly sliced onion
1 tablespoon kosher or coarse sea salt (about 2.5% of the weight of the vegetables)
2 teaspoons light brown sugar (1% of the weight of the vegetables)
2½ tablespoons coarsely ground Korean red pepper (about 3% of the weight of the vegetables)
¼ cup (60 ml) water (10% of the weight of the vegetables)

EQUIPMENT ▸ Plastic gloves; 1 quart (1 liter) airtight jar
AGING ▸ 1 month in the refrigerator
STORAGE ▸ Keeps 2 weeks refrigerated, 2 months frozen

1 Grate the garlic and ginger into a large bowl, then add the cabbage, daikon and onion.

2 Add the salt, sugar and red pepper. Put on the plastic gloves and knead the contents of the bowl until thoroughly combined.

3 Transfer the cabbage mixture to the storage jar. Add the water and mix to evenly distribute. Close the jar.

4 Store the kimchi in the refrigerator for one month before consuming. After 2 months the spiciness will mellow and the tartness will be enhanced.

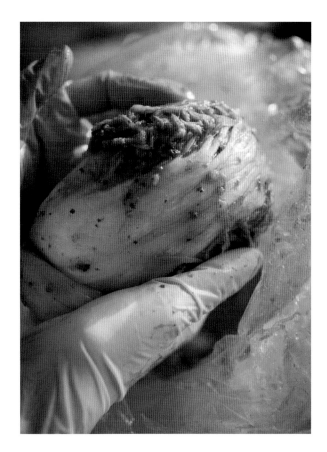

SERVING SUGGESTION
Kimchi Fried Rice

The key to making delicious kimchi fried rice is to start by stir-frying chopped kimchi in sesame oil and then add other ingredients such as diced onion, carrot, celery, green peas and finally day-old rice. You can top with a fried egg, sunny side up.

SERVING SUGGESTION
Kimchi Hotpot

Kimchi is great in a hotpot. Adding some of the juice deepens the flavor and you don't need much else in the way of seasoning. To prepare a hotpot for four people, add 4 oz (115 g) of Napa cabbage kimchi cut into bite-size pieces and ¾ cup (180 ml) of the juice to the pan. Include tofu, scallions, bean sprouts and pork or chicken meatballs for a hearty meal.

Honey Daikon Kimchi

Honey is the key to this kimchi, softening the spiciness of the daikon radish.

YIELDS: 1 lb (450 g)
PREPARATION TIME: 45 minutes using already-prepared Kimchi Seasoning Paste

1 daikon radish, about 2 lbs (1 kg), peeled and cut into 1 in (2.5cm) cubes
1 tablespoon kosher or coarse sea salt (3% of the weight of the daikon)
⅓ cup (100 g) Kimchi Seasoning Paste (see page 45) (10% of the weight of the daikon)
2 tablespoons honey
1 tablespoon roasted white sesame seeds

EQUIPMENT ▸ 1 gallon (4 liter) storage bag; 2 metal trays; weights totaling 2 lbs (1 kg)
AGING ▸ 1 day in a cool, dark place; 1 day in the refrigerator
STORAGE ▸ Keeps 10 days in the refrigerator

1 Put the daikon cubes and salt in the bag. Use your hands to massage the bag and mix the contents well. Seal the bag and place in a metal tray. Place a second metal tray on top of the bag and add the weight. Put the trays in a cool, dark place for 1 day.

2 Drain the water from the bag and remove the daikon. Wipe the water from the inside of the bag. Put the cubes back into the bag and add the Kimchi Seasoning Paste, honey and sesame seeds. Gently massage the bag to mix the contents.

3 Expel the air from the bag and seal it. Put the bag into the refrigerator for 1 day.

Cherry Tomato Kimchi

This unique kimchi contains a combination of sweet, sour and spicy flavors. Little holes in the skins of these tomatoes are the secret to good results.

YIELDS: 8 oz (225 g)
PREPARATION TIME: 15 minutes, using already-prepared Kimchi Seasoning Paste

8 oz (225 g) cherry tomatoes
1½ tablespoons Kimchi Seasoning Paste (see page 45) (15% of the weight of the cherry tomatoes)

CONTAINER ▸ 1 gallon (4 liter) storage bag
AGING ▸ 12 hours in the refrigerator
STORAGE ▸ Keeps 1 week in the refrigerator

1 Remove the stems from the cherry tomatoes. Use a toothpick to make holes in several places on each tomato.

2 Put the tomatoes and Kimchi Seasoning Paste in the bag and use your hands to gently massage the bag to mix the contents.

3 Expel the air from the bag and seal it. Put the bag into the refrigerator for 12 hours.

Bell Pepper Kimchi

This kimchi is ready overnight. Pickling bell peppers in this way brings out their sweetness.

YIELDS: 6 oz (170 g)
PREPARATION TIME: 15 minutes, using already-prepared Kimchi Seasoning Paste

8 oz (225 g) red and yellow bell peppers
1½ tablespoons Kimchi Seasoning Paste (see page 45) (20% of the weight of the bell peppers)

CONTAINER ▸ 1 gallon (4 liter) resealable storage bag
AGING ▸ 12 hours in the refrigerator
STORAGE ▸ Keeps 1 week in the refrigerator

1 Remove the stems and seeds from the bell peppers and cut them into 4 to 6 vertical slices. Cut the slices into halves.

2 Put the bell pepper slices into the bag, add the Kimchi Seasoning Paste and use your hands to gently massage the bag to mix the contents.

3 Expel the air from the bag and seal it. Place the bag into the refrigerator for 12 hours.

Mustard Spinach Kimchi

This recipe is made using Japanese mustard spinach (*komatsuna*) but works well with other green leafy vegetables such as turnip greens, bok choy, kale or green cabbage.

YIELDS: 4 oz (115 g)
PREPARATION TIME: 15 minutes, using already-prepared Kimchi Seasoning Paste

Large bunch mustard spinach or other leafy greens, about 8 oz (225 g)
1 teaspoon kosher or coarse sea salt (3% of the weight of the mustard spinach)
1 tablespoon Kimchi Seasoning Paste (see page 45) (10% of the weight of the mustard spinach)

CONTAINER ▸ 1 gallon (4 liter) storage bag
AGING ▸ 12 hours in the refrigerator
STORAGE ▸ Keeps 10 days in the refrigerator

1 Trim the ends of the greens. Fill a large bowl with water, add the greens and agitate to remove any dirt. Drain and pat dry with paper towels. Cut into 2-in (5-cm) lengths.

2 Put the greens in a mixing bowl. Sprinkle on the salt and set aside for about 1 hour.

3 Squeeze the liquid from the greens and put it into the bag. Add the Kimchi Seasoning Paste and gently massage the bag to mix the contents.

4 Expel the air from the bag and seal it. Put the bag into the refrigerator for 12 hours.

Honey Daikon Kimchi

Bell Pepper Kimchi

Mustard Spinach Kimchi

Cherry Tomato Kimchi

Refreshing White Kimchi

"White" kimchi contains no red chili pepper at all. With a bit of apple to provide sugar for fermentation, and either daikon radish or Napa cabbage as a starting point, add any combination of vegetables.

Bell Pepper and Cucumber White Kimchi

Celery and Turnip White Kimchi

Refreshing White Kimchi

This is a traditional Korean kimchi made by fermenting vegetables in water reserved from rinsing short grain rice. You can either make a pot of rice beforehand and reserve the rinsing water, or you can substitute rice flour mixed with water (see note below). This recipe is full of lactic acid bacteria, which is great for gut health. The liquid can be used to season other dishes.

YIELDS: 8 oz (225 g)
PREPARATION TIME: 45 minutes

2 cups (500 ml) water from rinsed rice (see note, below)
1 teaspoon sugar
1 lb (450 g) Napa cabbage, daikon radish, carrots and
   Japanese cucumber
1 tablespoon kosher or coarse sea salt
½ medium apple, cored and sliced (peel on)
1 garlic clove, mashed
2-in (5-cm) knob ginger, peeled and sliced

EQUIPMENT ▸ 1½ quart (1.5 liter) airtight storage container; plastic wrap
AGING ▸ 3 days in a cool, dark place
STORAGE ▸ Keeps 2 weeks in the refrigerator.

1 Put the reserved rice water and sugar in a saucepan and bring to a boil over medium heat. Remove from the heat.

2 Roughly chop the Napa cabbage. Peel and cut the daikon and carrots into bite-size rectangles. Halve the cucumber and cut it into thin diagonal slices. Place all the vegetables into a large shallow dish.

3 Salt the vegetables and set aside for 30 minutes.

4 Drain the liquid from the vegetables. Transfer the vegetables to the storage container. Add the apple, garlic and ginger.

5 Put the cooled rice water and sugar solution in the storage container. Place a sheet of plastic wrap directly on top of the vegetables. Seal the container. If making in winter, put the container in a cool, dark place for 3 days. At other times of the year put the container in a cool, dark place for 1 to 2 days then transfer to the refrigerator. In the lower photo, the left-hand container has just been prepared for aging. The right-hand container has aged for 3 days. When the liquid in the container has turned cloudy and there are bubbles in it, taste it. If it tastes a bit sour, the kimchi is ready to eat.

VARIATIONS
Try making Refreshing White Kimchi with bell pepper and cucumber (facing page, top), or with celery and turnip (facing page, center). For each, simply combine the pairs of vegetables for a total of 1 lb (450 g). The other ingredients and amounts are the same. Try using Asian pear instead of apple for a slightly lighter taste.

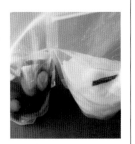

SERVING SUGGESTION
Chilled Summer Noodles

The mild tartness of the liquid from Refreshing White Kimchi is perfect for chilled noodles. Make the soup stock by combining equal amounts of chicken stock and kimchi liquid.

NOTE Short grain rice is rinsed multiple times. Reserve the water from the second rinsing. If you don't have reserved rice water, add 1 teaspoon (nonglutinous) rice flour to 2 cups (500 ml) of water in a saucepan. Bring to a boil. Remove from the heat and let cool to room temperature.

Pickled Plums

Japanese pickled plums, known as *umeboshi*, are made from the ume plum, which is actually a variety of apricot. Pickled plums, ubiquitous in the Japanese diet and most often eaten with rice, are made by brining, then drying in the sun, then aging for several months to a year and beyond, before consumption. When ready, the plums are wrinkled, supple, supremely sour and boast a variety of health benefits, among which are aiding digestion and controlling nausea.

This recipe has a salt content of only 17 percent. Use mature plums and add red shiso leaves for color. The availability of these plums will vary depending on your location. Generally they will make an appearance from late spring to early summer at Japanese and Korean groceries. Plan and order ahead. Their quantities are limited and they disappear fast. See the glossary on page 13 for more information about sourcing plums.

Schedule for Making Pickled Plums

Plum-preserving season begins in June in Japan. The following pages will take you through the three stages of plum-pickling: brining, preparing the shiso leaves and drying the plums.

EARLY TO LATE JUNE

Brining the Plums

During this stage, mature yellow plums are coated with salt and put into a container with a weight on top. Within several days to a week, a clear liquid, plum brine (umezu), will begin to accumulate. This liquid will be skimmed from the surface periodically and used for other purposes in the pickling process. See page 54.

LATE JUNE TO EARLY JULY

Pickling the Red Shiso Leaves

Red shiso leaves give pickled plums their characteristic red color. First the leaves are salted and kneaded to remove bitterness. Then they are placed into a mixing bowl and plum brine is added. This causes the leaves to redden. The leaves are added to the container of brined plums. See page 55. You can skip this stage if you don't want red plums (see note on Salt Cured Plums, below).

LATE JULY TO EARLY AUGUST

Drying the Plums

In Japan the end of July concludes the rainy season and sunshine is in the forecast—the ideal time for drying the brined plums. This period even has a name: *doyoboshi*. When 3 consecutive days of sunny weather are expected, the plums and red shiso (if using) are removed from the brine and dried outdoors on bamboo or rattan baskets or mats for good air circulation. See page 53.

HOW TO CHOOSE PLUMS

To make umeboshi pickled plums, use mature fruit, which should be mostly yellow in color. Set aside to ripen for a few days if necessary. Green, unripe plums will have a texture that is too hard for this recipe—use them to make Plum Liqueur (page 70) or Plum Syrup (page 71). The best Japanese varieties for making pickled plums are Nanko, Shirokaga and Togoro, all of which are thin-skinned and meaty. Experiment with what is available in your area, and see the Glossary of Ingredients on page 13 for more information.

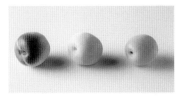

Selecting
Plums change from green to yellow as they mature and may have some red coloring.

Ripening
To ripen green plums, spread on a flat basket or in a cardboard box and place them by a sunny window. Check daily to prevent over-ripening.

Damaged Skins
For pickling, avoid plums with damaged skins, which can spoil the pickles. Cut off the damaged area and use the remaining flesh to make Miso Marinated Plums (page 60).

MAKING SALT CURED PLUMS

Salt Cured Plums (*shiraboshi-ume*) are pickled plums made following the steps on the following pages but without adding red shiso leaves, so they retain their tawny color. You can use them in a variety of recipes, including Honey Pickled Plums (see page 59).

Brining the Plums

Making pickled plums won't challenge your skills but may challenge your patience, with multiple steps to go through before you can set the plums aside to age in the dark and let time work its magic. This recipe uses less salt than traditional recipes in a nod to modern health concerns, but still ensures a long shelf life.

YIELDS: approx 2 lbs (1 kg)
PREPARATION TIME: 1 hour

4 lbs (1.8 kg) mature plums
½ cup (125 ml) white distilled liquor (35%, or 70 proof alcohol, Japanese shochu, vodka, etc.), plus more for sanitizing container
1⅓ cups (350 g) kosher or coarse sea salt (17% of the weight of the plums)

EQUIPMENT ▸ Bamboo skewer or toothpick; large, deep rectangular dish; 2 gallon (7.5 liter) wide-mouth ceramic, enamel, glass or plastic food-grade container; large, heavy-duty plastic bag to fit inside the container; drop lid or cover to fit inside the container; weights totaling 9 lbs (4 kg)

AGING ▸ 7–10 days in the refrigerator

CLEANING THE CONTAINER Wet a paper towel with distilled liquor and wipe the inside of the container.

 **1** Rinse the plums in a bowl or sink of water taking care not to damage the skins. Remove the plums and pat dry with paper towels. (If you have time, leaving the plums to soak in water for 2–3 hours before drying will improve the final taste).

 **2** Use a bamboo skewer or a toothpick to gently remove the disk of material atop the plum.

 **3** Place the plums in a large deep rectangular dish and pour the liquor over them. Gently stir.

 **4** Sprinkle a handful of salt evenly over the plums. Take care to salt the area at the stem.

 **5** Place a layer of salt on the bottom of the storage container and top with a single layer of plums. Sprinkle with salt. Continue until all the plums are in the container. Spread any remaining salt over the last layer.

 **6** Place a clean plastic bag in the container so that the bottom of the bag rests on the plums. Pull the open end of the bag down around the edge of the container. Place a drop lid or plate that fits snugly onto the bag. Place weights totaling 9 lbs (4 kg) on top. Cover the container and leave in a cool, dry place. Gently shake the container once a day. Plum vinegar will start emerging from the salted plums in about 3 days.

 **7** After 7–10 days, the plum vinegar will have risen to the top of the plums.

NOTE If you are making Salt Cured Plums (see page 53) without red shiso leaves, skim off the plum vinegar that rises to the top of the salted plums, leaving enough to just cover them. Reduce the weight to 4 lbs (2 kg). Cover the container and return to a cool, dark place until late July.

Pickling the Red Shiso Leaves

When the plum vinegar forms it is time to add the red shiso leaves that give the pickled plums a deep red color. Knead the leaves well as this will both remove bitterness and improve the flavor. (Skip this step if you're making the Salt Cured Plums described in the note on page 53).

YIELDS: 8 oz (225 g)
PREPARATION TIME: 30 minutes

16 oz (450 g) red shiso leaves
⅓ cup (80 g) kosher or coarse sea salt (20%
of the weight of the red shiso leaves)
4 tablespoons plum vinegar (see step 1 of
the recipe below), or rice vinegar

EQUIPMENT ▸ Tray or basket for drying the leaves; plastic gloves; large, heavy-duty plastic bag to fit inside the container; weights totaling 4 lbs (2 kg); drop lid or flat plate to fit inside the container
AGING ▸ 1 month in the refrigerator

1 Remove the cover, weights and plastic bag from the container holding the brined plums. Skim about 4 tablespoons of plum vinegar from the top of the plums, place in a bowl and set aside. While still attached to the sprig, rinse the shiso leaves and shake off excess water. With scissors, cut each leaf where it meets the stem. On a tray or basket spread the leaves out to briefly dry.

2 Wearing plastic gloves, put the leaves in a mixing bowl and sprinkle on a quarter of the salt. Knead the leaves until they soften.

3 A muddy-colored liquid will leach from the leaves. Continue kneading until a small pool collects in the bowl. Discard the liquid and repeat this step twice more.

4 Add the remaining salt and knead the leaves to squeeze out more liquid, which should become a clear purple color.

5 Squeeze out as much liquid as possible.

6 Transfer the leaves to another bowl, add the reserved plum vinegar or rice vinegar and knead the leaves until the liquid turns bright red.

7 Strain the red liquid from step 6 into the container of brined plums. Cover the top of the plums with the kneaded shiso leaves.

8 Place a plastic bag so that the bottom of the bag rests on the plums. Pull the open end of the bag down around the edge of the container. Place the drop lid or plate onto the bag and put weights totaling 4 lbs (2 kg) on top. Cover the container. Keep in a cool, dark place until late July, about 1 month.

Sun Drying the Plums

The process of making pickled plums reaches its final stage in late July when it is time to sun-dry the plums. Having aged for about a month, the plums will have a deep red color. Plan to watch the weather and begin this step when there will be 3 consecutive days of sunshine. This can be done outdoors or inside by a sunny window that will get at least 4 or 5 hours of sun. The plums will need to be turned periodically to maintain a nice circular shape.

EQUIPMENT ▸ Flat drying basket (bamboo or plastic);
  1 quart (1 liter) nonreactive strong container for the plum vinegar;
  1½ quart (1.5 liter) storage container for the plums
DRYING TIME ▸ 3 days
STORAGE ▸ Ready to eat after 1 month's storage; keeps indefinitely

HOW TO DRY THE PLUMS

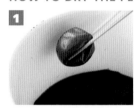

1 Remove the shiso leaves from the container, squeezing out the liquid. (The liquid should be squeezed back into the container—this is now red plum vinegar and it should be reserved until step 4.) Set the leaves aside. Remove the plums from the container and place them on a drying basket. This step should also be performed for the Salt Cured Plums without shiso (see page 53). Transfer the vinegar that has formed to the 1 quart container.

2 Space the plums evenly on the drying basket. Do the same for the red shiso leaves.

3 Place the basket outside in the sun or by a sunny window for 4–5 hours a day. Slightly elevate the baskets so air will circulate around the plums. Turn the plums periodically. If drying outdoors, bring the basket in at night.

4 On the second day, dip the plums in the reserved plum vinegar and then return to the basket. This imparts a moist texture. Keep turning the plums periodically. Repeat this step on the third day.

5 By the end of the third day, the plums should feel dry on the surface. Transfer them to the storage container. Add as much of the dried red shiso as you like. Reserve some of the leaves to make Tangy Red Leaf Powder (see this page).

Storage

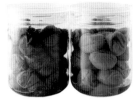

Store the plums in a cool, dark place. At this point, the plums are edible, but will be very sour. Waiting at least a month will mellow the sourness. Pickled plums are often aged for at least 6 months, often 1 year, before consuming.

Optional: Adding the reserved plum vinegar to cover the pickled plums will produce a moister, softer texture.

Aging the Plums

Pickled plums improve as they age. It is not uncommon to age them for 2 to 3 years or more. The longer they age, the more the salty sourness will mellow.

Top to bottom: freshly made, 3 years old, 7 years old and 10 years old. Pickled plums aged for 10 years become bundles of umami. Set aside a batch of your homemade pickled plums each year for further aging. Enjoy the tastes that evolve over time.

Tangy Red Shiso Powder

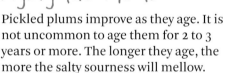

Reserve some of the red shiso leaves after drying. Use a food mill or mortar and pestle to make purple sour-salty powder. Sprinkle on rice and salads. Add to dressings or even dust a batch of cookies.

Plum Vinegar

Place a jar of plum vinegar in the sun for 4 to 5 hours. Sunlight will sterilize the vinegar and brighten its color. Store the jar in a cool, dark place.

Pickled Plums in a Bag

Use a heavy-duty resealable bag to make smaller amounts of pickled plums. Preparation methods for brining the plums and the red shiso leaves (if using) are the same as described on pages 54–55.

YIELDS: 1 lb (450 g)
PREPARATION TIME: 45 minutes

2 lbs (1 kg) mature plums
⅔ cup (170 g) kosher or coarse sea salt (17% of the weight of the plums)
4 tablespoons white distilled liquor (35%, 70 proof alcohol)

Pickled Red Shiso Leaves
8 oz (225 g) red shiso leaves
3 tablespoons kosher or coarse sea salt
2 tablespoons plum or rice vinegar

EQUIPMENT ▸ Bamboo skewer or toothpick; 1 gallon (4 liter) resealable plastic storage bag; metal tray or baking sheet; weights totaling 4 lbs (2 kg); parchment paper; 1 quart (1 liter) storage container
AGING ▸ 1 week to 10 days in the refrigerator
STORAGE ▸ Keeps 6 months in a cool, dark place

1 Follow steps 1–4 of Brining the Plums on page 54. In this case use the salt all at once. Place the plums in the storage bag, which should be big enough to spread the plums out in a single layer when laid flat.

2 Lay the bag flat on a baking sheet or tray large enough to hold the plums in a single layer. Place 4 lbs (2 kg) of weight on top of it. Jostle the tray once a day. Plum vinegar will begin to emerge on about the third day. After 7 to 10 days, there should be enough liquid to cover the plums.

3 Prepare the Pickled Red Shiso Leaves (see page 55). Add the red shiso leaves to the storage bag.

4 Return the bag to the metal tray and place 2 lbs (1 kg) of weight on top of it (**photo A**). Set the tray aside for about 1 month.

5 After a month, line a baking sheet or tray with parchment paper. Open the bag, remove the leaves and squeeze out the liquid, which can be reserved as plum vinegar. Remove the plums and place them on the tray. Space out the plums and leaves evenly.

6 Place the tray by a sunny window for 4 to 5 hours a day (**photo B**) for 3 days. Transfer the plums to a storage container. Keep in a cool, dark place for one month.

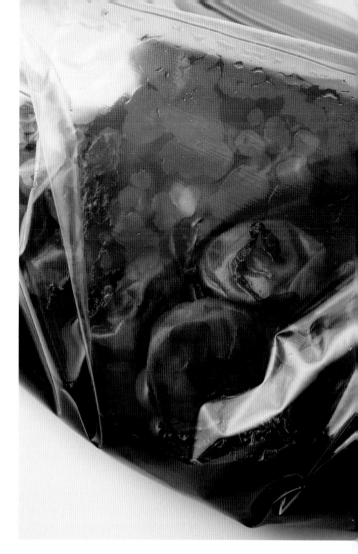

NOTES AND TIPS You can use the storage bag for aging. The plums will retain some moisture even after drying which makes for a soft texture. If you can find ready-to-use preserved red shiso leaves (see Glossary of Ingredients, page 14) for use in making pickled plums, this will simplify the process.

Japanese Pickled Plums as a Seasoning

The aroma, beautiful color and salty-sour flavor of Japanese pickled plums and plum vinegar make for excellent seasonings, with health benefits. The plums contain antimicrobial substances that help to stave off spoilage, and their sour flavor stimulates the appetite and helps relieve fatigue.

Rice with Pickled Plums and Anchovies

A pickled plum in every pot

For a refreshing rice dish, add one umeboshi pickled plum to the rice pot for every cup of rice. When the rice is done, fold in some *chirimenjako* whitebait, cooked edamame and roasted white sesame seeds.
If you can't find chirimenjako at your Japanese market, chopped walnut has a similar texture.

Sardines Simmered with Pickled Plums

Pickled plums reduce the smell of fish

Put 2 tablespoons soy sauce, 2 tablespoons sake, 1 tablespoon sugar, 1 tablespoon mirin and 1 cup (250 ml) water in a pan. Add ginger slices and 1 umeboshi pickled plum per person. Bring to a boil and add the sardines. Cook until the flesh is firm to the touch and the sauce has been reduced. Mackerel and bluefish fillets can be prepared in the same manner.

Somen Noodles with Pickled Plums

For hot summer days

Sake-steamed chicken breast, boiled okra stars, sliced scallions, a green shiso leaf and a pickled plum are a great combination of toppings for cold somen noodles. Take small bites of plum with every mouthful.

Blushing Chirashizushi

Pink sushi rice!

Make a dressing of 3 parts plum vinegar and 1 part sugar. Add to cooked short-grain white rice to make pink-tinted sushi rice. Mix in tuna flakes, salted cucumber and strips of shio kombu salted kelp or vegetables of your choice. Top with scrambled-egg crumbles.

Honey Pickled Plums

This pleasantly sweet and salty soft plum goes perfectly with a cup of green tea.

YIELDS: approx 8 oz (225 g)
PREPARATION TIME: 30 minutes

Water for soaking
1 lb (450 g) Salt Cured Plums (see page 53)
1⅓ cups (450 g) honey
1 cup (250 ml) water

CONTAINER ▸ 1 quart (1 liter) airtight storage jar
AGING ▸ 2 weeks in the refrigerator
STORAGE ▸ Keeps 3 months in the refrigerator

1 Fill a large bowl with water. Add the plums and soak for about 12 hours.

2 Put the honey and the water in a medium saucepan and bring to a boil over medium heat. Remove from the heat and allow to cool to room temperature.

3 Have on hand the prepared storage jar. Drain the water from the plums and dry each plum with a paper towel. Put the plums into the storage jar. Pour the cooled honey-and-water solution over the plums. Put the jar in the refrigerator to marinate for 2 weeks before using.

Miso Marinated Plums

Marinating mature plums in a slightly sweet miso mellows the flavors. Make a paste from the meat of the marinated plums and the miso for a tasty topping for chilled tofu.

YIELDS: 6 oz (170 g)
PREPARATION TIME: 35 minutes

3 large ripe plums
½ cup (150 g) miso
5 tablespoons light brown sugar

EQUIPMENT ▸ Bamboo skewer or toothpick;
  1 pint (500 ml) storage container
AGING ▸ 1 month in the refrigerator
STORAGE ▸ Keeps 6 months in the refrigerator

NOTE If you have leftover miso after finishing the plums, you can use it as a seasoning for other dishes.

1 Fill the sink or a plastic tub with water. Add the plums and carefully rinse to avoid damaging the skins. Remove the plums and pat dry with paper towels. Use a bamboo skewer or a toothpick to gently remove the disk of material atop the plum.

2 In a mixing bowl, combine the miso and sugar and mix well. Spoon half the mixture into the storage container. Place the plums on top of the miso mixture. Spread the remaining mixture on top of the plums (**photo A**).

3 Store the container in the refrigerator for 1 month. The container will fill with liquid that has leached from the plums. Do not remove the liquid (**photo B**).

Plums Pickled in Shio Koji

Shio koji is a natural seasoning made of salt, water and rice malt. Ripe plums aged in shio koji for 1 month are wonderful on their own or as an ingredient in vegetable dressings.

YIELDS: 2 cups (500 ml)
PREPARATION TIME: 15 minutes

5 large ripe plums
¾ cup (300 g) shio koji paste (150% of the weight of the plums)

EQUIPMENT ▶ Bamboo skewer or toothpick; 1 pint (500 ml) airtight storage jar
AGING ▶ 1 month in the refrigerator
STORAGE ▶ Keeps 6 months in the refrigerator

1 Fill the sink or a plastic tub with water. Add the plums and carefully rinse to avoid damaging the skins. Remove the plums and pat dry with paper towels. Use a bamboo skewer or a toothpick to gently remove the disk of material atop the plum.

2 Put the plums into the jar and add the shio koji paste. (**photo A**). Store the jar in the refrigerator. The jar will fill with liquid that has leached from the plums (**photo B**). Do not discard the liquid. The plums are ready to eat after 1 month.

Sweet Apple Cider Plums

Cutting the plums in half lessens the time needed for aging and results in a delightfully crisp texture.

YIELDS: approx 8 oz (225 g)
PREPARATION TIME: 45 minutes

1 lb (450 g) green plums
1¾ tablespoons kosher or coarse sea salt (approx 5% of the weight of the plums after pitting)
1 tablespoon apple cider vinegar
1¾ cups (350 g) granulated sugar

EQUIPMENT ▶ Bamboo skewer or toothpick; 2 cutting boards; plastic wrap; small bowl to use as weight; 1 quart (1 liter) storage jar
AGING ▶ 10 days in the refrigerator
STORAGE ▶ Keeps 6 months in the refrigerator

1 Fill the sink or a plastic tub with water. Add the plums and carefully rinse to avoid damaging the skins. Remove the plums and pat dry with paper towels. Use a bamboo skewer or a toothpick to gently remove the disk of material atop the plum.

2 With a sharp paring knife, slit the plum from top to bottom, along the seam and around the pit. Do not pull apart. Repeat for each plum.

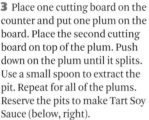

3 Place one cutting board on the counter and put one plum on the board. Place the second cutting board on top of the plum. Push down on the plum until it splits. Use a small spoon to extract the pit. Repeat for all of the plums. Reserve the pits to make Tart Soy Sauce (below, right).

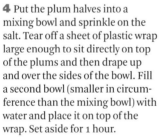

4 Put the plum halves into a mixing bowl and sprinkle on the salt. Tear off a sheet of plastic wrap large enough to sit directly on top of the plums and then drape up and over the sides of the bowl. Fill a second bowl (smaller in circumference than the mixing bowl) with water and place it on top of the wrap. Set aside for 1 hour.

5 Remove the second bowl and the plastic wrap and strain the liquid that has accumulated around the plum halves. Pour the apple cider vinegar evenly onto the plums. The vinegar inhibits the growth of unwanted microorganisms.

6 Place some of the plums into the jar and sprinkle on a little of the sugar. Layer the plums and sugar in this way until all the sugar and all the plums are in the jar. Store the jar in the refrigerator for about 10 days.

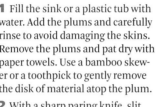

7 Periodically shake the jar to ensure the plum halves are evenly coated with the sugar.

8 At the end of 10 days, the plums will have shrunk, losing most of their water content. Keep the plums stored in this marinade. The marinade can be used in recipes calling for sweet vinegar.

Plum Infused Soy Sauce

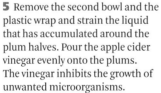

Use the reserved pits from green plums to impart a refreshing tartness to soy sauce. Weigh the pits and place in a clean glass jar. Cover the pits with twice that weight in soy sauce. Store the jar in a cool, dark place for about 2 weeks. This soy sauce will keep for about 3 months in the refrigerator.

Plums in a Shiso Blanket

Magenta shiso leaves wrapped around crunchy plum halves make this a treat for the eyes and the palate.

YIELDS: 30 pieces
PREPARATION TIME: 1 hour

For the leaves

30 red shiso leaves
½ teaspoon kosher or coarse sea salt (20% of the weight of the red shiso leaves)
4 tablespoons water
4 tablespoons plum vinegar, or rice vinegar

For the plums

15 green plums, about 12 oz (350 g)
½ cup (100 g) granulated sugar (about 50% of the weight of the plums after pitting)
1½ tablespoons kosher or coarse sea salt (about 3% of the weight of the plums after pitting)

EQUIPMENT ▸ 2 nesting metal trays; plastic wrap; plastic gloves; 2 cutting boards; 1 flat storage container; weights totaling 1–1½ lbs (500–700 g)
AGING ▸ 1 month in the refrigerator
STORAGE ▸ Keeps 3 months in the refrigerator

1 Rinse the shiso leaves under running water. Shake off the excess water. With scissors, cut the leaves from their stems. Place half of the leaves on the bottom of a metal tray and sprinkle on a third of the salt.

2 Pour on half of the water, then add the remaining shiso leaves. Sprinkle on half of the remaining salt and then pour on the rest of the water.

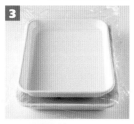

3 Place a sheet of plastic wrap directly on top of the shiso leaves. The sheet should be big enough to cover the sides of the tray. Fill a second metal tray, that fits inside the first tray, with water and place it on top of the wrap. Set aside for 2 hours.

4 Remove the top tray and discard the water. Wearing gloves, press down on the shiso leaves to force out the liquid. Pick up the bundle of leaves and gently squeeze to extract more liquid.

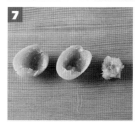

5 Spread the leaves open and sprinkle on the remaining salt. Knead the leaves gently, taking care not to tear them. Roll up the leaves and squeeze out the liquid.

6 Set the leaves on a clean plate and rinse the tray. Spread the leaves out on the tray and add the plum vinegar. The leaves will change color.

7 Split the green plums as described in steps 2–3 on page 62. In a bowl mix the sugar and salt.

8 Discard the vinegar from the tray in step 6. Take a shiso leaf and lay it out flat. Place 2 plum halves on the leaf at the stem edge. Fold the sides of the leaf over the plums and roll the leaf up, cigar style. Repeat until all the leaves are used and line them up next to each other in the tray.

9 Sprinkle the rolls with the sugar and salt mixture. Place a sheet of plastic wrap directly on top of the rolls with enough wrap to go over the sides of the tray. Place a weight on top of the wrap. Store the tray in the refrigerator for 1 month. Remove the weight. The pickles are ready to eat.

Crunchy Pickled Plums

The Japanese word for crunchy is *kari-kari* and that's just how it sounds when you bite into these young plum pickles. Steeping an eggshell in the pickling vinegar adds calcium.

YIELDS: 1 lb (450 g)
PREPARATION TIME: 45 minutes

Water for soaking
2 lbs (1 kg) small green plums
Shells from 2 eggs, sundried for an hour and membrane removed
⅔ cup (150 ml) plum or rice vinegar
½ cup (125 ml) white distilled liquor (35%, or 70 proof, alcohol)
½ cup (120 g) kosher or coarse sea salt (12% of the weight of the plums)

For the Pickled Red Shiso Leaves
8 oz (225 g) red shiso leaves
3 tablespoons kosher or coarse sea salt
2 tablespoons plum or rice vinegar

EQUIPMENT ▸ Tea filter bag; bamboo skewer or toothpick; 3 sturdy resealable 1 gallon (4 liter) plastic bags; 1½ quart (1.5 liter) storage jar; plastic gloves; 1 pint (500 ml) storage jar
AGING ▸ 1 week in a cool, dark place or the refrigerator
STORAGE ▸ Keeps 3 months in the refrigerator

PREPARING THE INGREDIENTS

Fill a bowl large enough to hold all the plums with water. Add the plums and soak for 1 hour.

Meanwhile crush the eggshells into fine pieces and put them into a tea filter bag. Put the vinegar in a small pan and the bag of eggshells.

Bring the pan to a boil and remove from the heat. Let cool to room temperature and remove the bag of eggshells.

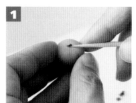

1 Remove the plums from the bowl of water and pat dry with paper towels. With a bamboo skewer or toothpick, remove the disk of material where the stem was attached.

2 Put the plums in a large mixing bowl and pour in the liquor to cover evenly. This inhibits the development of mold.

3 Discard the liquor and transfer the plums to a plastic bag. Add the salt. Place the bag on a flat surface. With one hand holding the bag closed, use your other hand to roll the plums around in the salt. This scratches the skins, which stops the plums from further ripening and maintains a crisp texture.

4 Roll the plums until the salt has mostly dissolved. Transfer the plums to the larger storage jar.

5 Pour the cooled vinegar into the same plastic bag that held the plums. Swish around to rinse the salt from the inside of the bag and then pour over the plums.

6 Fill a new 1 quart (1 liter) resealable plastic bag with water and seal the bag. Place this bag into another bag and seal that bag. Put the doubled bag of water on top of the plums in the jar. Close the jar and keep in a cool, dark place for about 1 week. Periodically tilt the jar in various directions to evenly coat all the plums.

7 Follow steps 1–6 on page 55 to prepare the pickled red shiso leaves. Skip if you prefer not to give the plums a red color.

8 After the plums have aged for a week, transfer them to the smaller jar. If using red shiso leaves, drain and squeeze the liquid from them and add to the jar. (Reserve the vinegar from the leaves in a separate jar for use in other recipes.) Place the jar in the refrigerator for 1 week before consuming.

Young Plums in Soy Sauce

Ready in just a week, these young green plums are marinated in soy sauce and get a flavor boost from a strip of kombu. They are great with a bowl of rice.

YIELDS: 2 cups (500 ml)
PREPARATION TIME: 25 minutes

8 oz (225 g) young green plums
¾ cup (180 ml) soy sauce
1 piece dried kombu seaweed, 2 in (5 cm) square

EQUIPMENT ▸ Bamboo skewer or toothpick; 1 pint (500 ml) storage jar
AGING ▸ 1 week in a cool, dark place
STORAGE ▸ Keeps 6 months in the refrigerator

1 Fill the sink or a plastic tub with water. Add the plums and carefully rinse to avoid damaging the skins. Remove the plums and pat dry with paper towels. Use a bamboo skewer or a toothpick to gently remove the disk of material atop the plum.

2 Put the plums in the jar and add the soy sauce and kombu. Close the jar and store in a cool, dark place for 1 week. Periodically tilt the jar to ensure the plums are evenly exposed to the soy sauce.

Young Plums in Shio Koji

Young green plums marinate in shio-koji rice-malt seasoning for only a week to give plums with a soft texture and surprisingly delicious flavor.

YIELDS: 2 cups (500 ml)
PREPARATION TIME: 25 minutes

8 oz (225 g) young green plums
½ cup (200 g) shio koji paste

EQUIPMENT ▸ Bamboo skewer or toothpick; 1 pint (500 ml) airtight storage jar
AGING ▸ 1 week in a cool, dry place
STORAGE ▸ Keeps 6 months in the refrigerator

1 Fill the sink or a plastic tub with water. Add the plums and carefully rinse to avoid damaging the skins. Remove the plums and pat dry with paper towels. Use a bamboo skewer or a toothpick to gently remove the disk of material atop the plum.

2 Put the plums into the jar and add the shio koji paste. Close the jar and keep in a cool, dark place for 1 week. Periodically tilt the jar to ensure the plums are evenly coated.

> **NOTE** The liquid that is produced from all three of the recipes on this page can be used as seasoning for other dishes.

Sweet Young Pickled Plums

Wrinkled from marinating in salt and sugar for a week, these plums aren't winning any beauty contests. But don't let looks fool you—they are delicious.

YIELDS: 1 quart (1 liter)
PREPARATION TIME: 25 minutes

12 oz (350 g) young green plums
2 tablespoons white distilled liquor (35%, or 70 proof, alcohol)
3 tablespoons kosher or coarse sea salt
½ cup (100g) sugar
1¼ cups (300 ml) water

EQUIPMENT ▸ Bamboo skewer or toothpick; 1 quart (1 liter) airtight storage jar; 2 x 1 quart (1 liter) resealable plastic bags
AGING ▸ 2 weeks in a cool, dark place
STORAGE Keeps 6 months in the refrigerator

1 Fill the sink or a plastic tub with water. Add the plums and carefully rinse to avoid damaging the skins. Remove the plums and pat dry with paper towels. Use a bamboo skewer or a toothpick to gently remove the disk of material atop the plum.

2 Place the plums in a mixing bowl and evenly pour over the liquor. Fold in the salt and sugar and mix until well coated.

3 Transfer the contents of the mixing bowl to the storage jar. Fill the plastic bag with the water and seal the bag. Place the bag into another bag and seal. Put the doubled bag of water on top of the plums in the jar. Close the jar and keep it in a cool, dark place for about 1 week.

4 The liquid that emerges from the plums is plum vinegar. Periodically tilt the jar to ensure the plums are evenly exposed to the liquid. When the plum vinegar covers the plums remove the bag of water. Keep the jar in a cool, dark place for an additional week.

Start with a jar filled with smooth plums and a bit of liquid. End with puckered plums and a jar full of liquid.

Young Plums Pickled in Soy Sauce

Sweet Young Pickled Plums

Plum Liqueur

The combination of green plums, white distilled liquor and rock sugar gives you a slightly sweet and light plum liqueur. Japanese shochu, alcohol distilled with sweet potatoes, rice, barley or brown sugar, is ideal for making plum liqueur but vodka also works well. Set to steep at summer's start and sip at the winter solstice. Plum liqueur grows mellower over time. Remove the fruit after a year to stop the liqueur from becoming cloudy. There is no expiration date. Enjoy for as long as it lasts!

YIELDS: 1 quart (1 liter)
PREPARATION TIME: 35 minutes

1 lb (450 g) green plums
8 oz (225 g) rock sugar
1 quart (1 liter) white distilled liquor (35%, or 70 proof, alcohol) plus more for disinfection

EQUIPMENT ▸ Bamboo skewer or toothpick; 1½ quart (1.5 liter) airtight storage jar
AGING ▸ 6 months in a cool, dry place
STORAGE ▸ Keeps indefinitely in a cool, dry place

1 Fill the sink or a plastic tub with water. Add the plums and carefully rinse to avoid damaging the skins. Remove the plums and pat dry with paper towels. Use a bamboo skewer or a toothpick to gently remove the disk of material atop the plum.

2 Put the plums, rock sugar and liquor into the jar.

3 Keep in a cool, dark place for at least 6 months, or until the plums all sink to the bottom of the jar. The liqueur is then ready to drink, but will continue to mellow with time.

CLEANING THE JAR
To disinfect the jar, add a small amount of the alcohol and close the lid. Swish the alcohol around the inside of the jar, then discard.

Plum Syrup

Green plum syrup diluted with cold water or club soda makes a refreshing drink. Apple cider vinegar extends the life of this syrup, which can easily begin to ferment in a warm room.

YIELDS: 1 quart (1 liter)
PREPARATION TIME: 45 minutes

White distilled alcohol for disinfecting (35%, or 70 proof, alcohol)
2 lbs (1 kg) green plums
2 lbs (1 kg) rock sugar
½ cup (125 ml) apple cider vinegar

EQUIPMENT ▸ Bamboo skewer or toothpick; 1½ quart (1.5 liter) airtight storage jar
AGING ▸ 1 month in the refrigerator
STORAGE ▸ Keeps 1 year in the refrigerator

1 Wet a paper towel with distilled liquor and wipe the inside of the jar and its lid.

2 Fill the sink or a plastic tub with water. Add the plums and carefully rinse to avoid damaging the skins. Remove the plums and pat dry with paper towels. Use a bamboo skewer or a toothpick to gently remove the disk of material atop the plum.

3 Lay several plums on the bottom of the jar to form a single layer. Add a layer of rock sugar. Repeat until you have used up the plums. Finish with a layer of rock sugar on top. Pour in the apple cider vinegar.

4 Store in a cool, dark place for 1 month. Periodically tilt the jar to mix the contents. Do this until the rock sugar is completely dissolved. If bubbles begin to form, indicating that fermentation is taking place, open the jar occasionally to let gas out. After 1 month, remove the plums from the jar and store in the refrigerator for up to 1 year.

Red Shiso Juice

Red shiso leaves add vibrant color to this juice. Dilute for beverages, or use as a topping for desserts.

YIELDS: 1 quart (1 liter)
PREPARATION TIME: 25 minutes

CONTAINER ▸ 1 quart (1 liter) storage jar
STORAGE ▸ Keeps 3 months in the refrigerator

12 oz (350 g) red shiso leaves
1 quart (1 liter) water
2 cups (400 g) granulated sugar
3 teaspoons citric acid granules or ½ cup (125 ml) apple cider vinegar

> **NOTE** Look for food-grade citric acid at a drugstore or online.

1 Rinse the red shiso leaves and shake off the excess water.

2 Put the water in a saucepan and bring to a boil over medium heat. Add the red shiso leaves and boil for about 5 minutes or until they turn green. Set a strainer over a mixing bowl and line with a paper towel. Pour the leaves and liquid through the strainer (**photo A**). Set the leaves aside.

3 Add the sugar to the strained liquid and mix until dissolved. Add the citric acid or vinegar (**photo B**). Let the liquid cool and transfer to the storage jar.

Chapter 2
Traditional Recipes

This chapter introduces a range of traditional Japanese pickles and regional favorites, all of which can be made in the home kitchen. Some require substantial aging, but as long as the recipe is correctly followed, your efforts will pay off with an authentic flavor.

Crunchy Daikon Pickles

Made from dried daikon radish, this is a very popular Japanese pickle known as *takuan*. In Japan, dried daikon are available in markets from the end of November to the beginning of December. They are generally pliable but if hard to bend by hand, try softening them in the sun for several days before using. Dried daikon may be difficult to source but with patience you can dry your own. See instructions opposite.

YIELDS: 2 lbs (1 kg) of pickles
PREPARATION TIME: 40 minutes

4 or 5 dried daikon, about 3 lbs (1.4 kg)
¼ cup (60g) kosher or coarse sea salt (6% of the weight of the dried daikon)

Pickling Bed
Handful of salt
1¾ cup (225 g) rice bran (15% of the weight of the dried daikon)
2 tablespoons coarse sugar (2% of the weight of the dried daikon)
1 dried red chili pepper, deseeded
1 piece dried kombu seaweed, 2 in × 4 in (5 × 10 cm)
Peel from ½ persimmon (dried 1 day in the sun)
Peel from ½ apple (dried 1 day in the sun)

EQUIPMENT ▸ 5 quart (5 liter) container; heavy duty plastic bag to fit inside the storage container; weights totaling 5 lbs (2.5 kg)
AGING ▸ 6 weeks in a cool, dry place
STORAGE ▸ Keeps 3 months in a cool, dry place

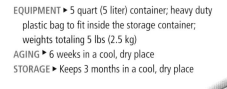

5 Use half of the remaining pickling bed to cover the bottom layer of daikon. Pack in the remaining daikon.

1 Cut the greens from the daikon and reserve. Remove any darkened or damaged parts from the daikon. Bend the daikon this way and that to make them more flexible and easier to pack into the storage container. Give them a quick rinse and let them drain.

6 Add the remainder of the pickling bed to cover the second layer of daikon. Press the pickling medium and daikon firmly into the container with your hands. Level off the surface and then sprinkle on the ¼ cup of salt.

2 To make the pickling bed, put the handful of salt into a mixing bowl, add the rest of the pickling bed ingredients and mix. The fruit peel will contribute a little bit of sweetness.

7 Use the daikon greens to form the top layer. Press the air out of the bag and seal the bag.

3 Line the storage container with a plastic bag. Add a third of the pickling bed and level off the top to create a flat surface in the container.

8 Place the weights on top of the bag and cover the container. Put the container in a cool, dark place for 10 days. When you notice that water has risen to the top of the bag, reduce the weight by half. (If water has not accumulated in the bag, add more weight, or make a 4% saltwater solution and pour this evenly onto the contents of the bag.) Leave for 1 more month.

9 When your pickles are ready, pull out only as much as you will eat that day. With your hands scrape the rice bran back into the container. To eat, slice into thin rounds as pictured opposite.

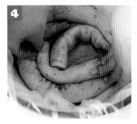

4 Put half of the daikon into the container by coiling and packing them as tightly as possible. It's okay to cut the daikon to do this.

DRY YOUR OWN DAIKON RADISHES

Purchase long, firm, thin daikon, if possible with leaves. You will be making a cradle for the daikon radishes with strong twine to hang outside to dry. This should be done in dry, sunny weather,

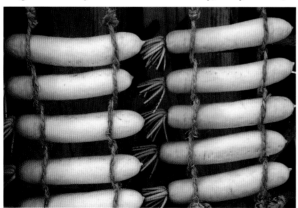

bringing the daikon in at night. You can also dry indoors in a sunny room with good air circulation. Drying takes 2 weeks or until they shrivel and are flexible enough to bend into an arc.

1 Lay one daikon on a table horizontally. Wrap strong twine around the daikon several times, about $\frac{1}{4}$ of the way from the top end. Do not cut the string. Place another daikon below the first daikon and, using the same twine as for the first daikon, wrap another several loops $\frac{1}{4}$ of way from the top end. You can add up to 2 more daikon radishes, continuing with the same piece of twine. Tie off.

2 Repeat the steps, starting with another string for the bottom ends of the daikon, creating a cradle of daikon radishes. Find a sunny place outside where you can hang the cradle for about 2 weeks.

3 Check periodically that the radishes are becoming pliable. They will be ready to place in the rice bran pickling bed when they are flexible enough to bend into the pickling bucket. Proceed with the recipe for Crunchy Daikon Pickles on the facing page.

Dried Daikon Pickles

The recipes on this page are made from *wariboshi* daikon, which is daikon radish that has been sliced lengthwise and dried. Wariboshi daikon is usually home-dried in Japan. Have a go yourself, following the steps on this page!

YIELDS: 12 oz (350 g)
PREPARATION TIME: 40 minutes

4 oz (115 g) wariboshi daikon strips
5 tablespoons soy sauce
4 tablespoons rice vinegar
3 tablespoons mirin
3 tablespoons light brown sugar
1 dried red chili pepper, deseeded
1 piece dried kombu seaweed, 2 in (5 cm) square

EQUIPMENT ▸ Heat-resistant mixing bowl; 1 quart (1 liter) resealable plastic bag
AGING ▸ 12 hours in the refrigerator
STORAGE ▸ Keeps 1 month in the refrigerator

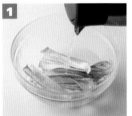

1 Put the wariboshi daikon in the heat-resistant mixing bowl and fill the bowl with boiling water. Let cool to room temperature, drain out the water and squeeze out as much water as you can from the daikon.

2 Transfer the daikon to a cutting board. Halve each piece and then cut into ½ in (1 cm) pieces. Put the daikon back into the heat-resistant mixing bowl.

3 Put all the other ingredients in a saucepan, bring to a boil and then pour the contents onto the wariboshi daikon pieces.

4 After the bowl has cooled, transfer the contents to the plastic bag. Expel the air from the bag, seal and put in the refrigerator for 12 hours.

Sweet and Crunchy Daikon Pickles

This version takes the crunch down a notch.

YIELDS: 12 oz (350 g)
PREPARATION TIME: 40 minutes

4 oz (115 g) wariboshi daikon strips
⅔ cup (150 ml) rice vinegar
4 tablespoons sugar
2 tablespoons light soy sauce
1 teaspoon kosher or coarse sea salt
1 dried red chili pepper, deseeded
1 piece dried kombu seaweed, 2 in (5 cm) square

EQUIPMENT ▸ Heat-resistant mixing bowl; 1 quart (1 liter) resealable plastic bag
AGING ▸ 12 hours in the refrigerator
STORAGE ▸ Keeps 1 month in the refrigerator

Follow the same recipe steps as for Dried Daikon Pickles, using a nonaluminum saucepan.

HOW TO MAKE DRIED WARIBOSHI DAIKON STRIPS

1 Cut a fresh daikon radish in half and then cut each half into long slices ½ in (1 cm) thick. Make a slit down the middle of each slice, leaving 1 in (2.5 cm) uncut at the narrower end.

2 Hang the daikon slices on clothes hangers outside. Bring the hangers in at night and on rainy days.

3 When the daikon feels dry to the touch and is reduced to about 10% of its original weight, it is sufficiently dried. This takes about 2 weeks. One fresh daikon should yield about 5 oz (150 g) of wariboshi daikon. It will keep in the refrigerator for about 6 months.

Sweet and Crunchy
Daikon Pickles

Dried Daikon Pickles

Cucumber "Plank" Pickles

Japanese cucumbers are small and thin with edible skin and are available at Asian markets. Persian, Armenian or mini cucumbers are good substitutes. The use of salt and a weight flattens the cucumbers, hence the nickname "plank" pickles. To make the delicious condiment, Aged Cucumber Pickles, shown in the photo opposite, mix chopped Cucumber "Plank" Pickles (that have been desalted, see note below) with small amounts of chopped fresh ginger, chopped green shiso leaves and Soy Cured Shiso Seeds (see page 127).

YIELDS: 1 lb (450 g)
PREPARATION TIME: 35 minutes

½ cup (100g) kosher or coarse sea salt (10% of the weight of the cucumbers)

2 lbs (1 kg) Japanese cucumbers

Brine
¾ cup (180 ml) water
1½ tablespoons kosher or coarse sea salt

1st addition: ½ cup (120 g) kosher or coarse sea salt
2nd addition: 3 tablespoons kosher or coarse sea salt

EQUIPMENT ▸ 5 quart (5 liter) container; 2 x 2 gallon (7.5 liter) resealable plastic bags; weights totaling 8–10 lbs (4–5kg)
AGING ▸ 6 weeks in a cool, dry place
STORAGE ▸ Keeps 6 months in a cool, dry place, or 1 year if you drain off the pickling solution and refrigerate

1 Spread a handful of the ½ cup of salt on the bottom of the container.

2 Pack a layer of cucumbers into the bottom of the container. Put another handful of salt on top.

3 Pack in another layer of cucumbers and spread with the remaining salt.

4 To make the brine, mix the water and the 1½ tablespoons of salt in a bowl. Pour the brine into the container around the outer edge of the cucumbers.

5 Put a plastic bag bottom first into the container, directly on top of the cucumbers, and open it up. Put the weights into the bag. Set the container aside in a cool, dark place for about 4 days.

6 After about four days, water will have risen in the container. Remove the weights and the bag. Sprinkle in the 1st addition of salt. Put the bag and the weight back in place and set the container aside for another week.

7 Remove the weights and the bag. Discard the brine and rinse the cucumbers and the container. The cucumbers will be relatively flat.

8 Return the cucumbers to the washed container. Sprinkle on the 2nd addition of salt and mix it into the cucumbers with your hands. Again, put a plastic bag into the container bottom first, on top of the cucumbers. Open the bag up and put the weights into the bag. Set the container aside for at least 1 month.

DESALTING THE PICKLES
When you want to eat the cucumbers, take out what you will consume and soak in plenty of water for at least 12 hours to reduce the salt. Change the water 2 or 3 times during the 12 hours. Sample the cucumbers as you desalt them. When you get the flavor you want, slice and enjoy.

REMOVING MOLD
As your cucumbers age, white dots of mold may develop. To remove it, pour the pickling solution through a filter into a saucepan and bring to a boil. Remove from the heat then let cool to room temperature. Rinse the container and the cucumbers in water, removing the mold. Return the cucumbers to the container and pour the pickling solution back in.

Cucumber "Plank" Pickles are the basis of this popular Japanese condiment, Aged Cucumber Pickles. See the headnote on the facing page for the recipe.

Spicy Hokkaido Pickles

These very spicy pickles are a traditional favorite on Japan's northernmost island of Hokkaido.

YIELDS: 10 oz (280 g)
PREPARATION TIME 35 minutes

4 green jalapeno peppers
1 cup (225 g) dried rice koji
¾ cup (180 ml) soy sauce

TOOLS ▶ Plastic gloves;
  1 pint (500 ml) storage
  container
AGING ▶ 10 days in a
  cool, dark place
STORAGE ▶ Keeps
  6 months in the
  refrigerator

2 Put the chopped peppers, rice koji and soy sauce in a bowl. Mix and then transfer to the storage container.

3 Set the container aside in a cool, dark place for at least 10 days, mixing periodically.

1 Wearing plastic gloves, remove the stems from the peppers and chop into small pieces. If you would like to reduce the heat a bit, halve the peppers and remove the seeds before chopping.

4 After about 10 days, the liquid in the container will have thickened a bit and your spicy pickles will be ready to eat. This is a wonderful accompaniment to a bowl of rice!

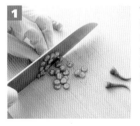

Matsumae Seafood Pickles

The seaside town of Matsumae in Hokkaido, makes the most of local seafood produce for these pickles, which contain kombu seaweed, cuttlefish and herring roe.

YIELDS: 2 cups (300 g)
PREPARATION TIME: 35 minutes

2 small carrots
Handful kiriboshi daikon strips
2 tablespoons sake
3 tablespoons mirin
2 oz (50 g) dried kombu seaweed
3 pieces whole pickled herring roe (desalted)
Handful shredded dried cuttlefish
1 dried red chili pepper, deseeded
1 tablespoon light brown sugar
4 tablespoons soy sauce
6 tablespoons water

CONTAINER ▶ 1 quart (1 liter) resealable storage bag
AGING ▶ 2 hours in a cool, dark place
STORAGE ▶ Keeps 1 month in the refrigerator

1 Peel and julienne the carrots. Rehydrate the dried daikon strips and then squeeze out the excess water.

2 Put the sake and mirin in a saucepan and bring to a boil. Remove from the heat, add the sugar, soy sauce and water and leave to cool.

3 Julienne the kombu and break the herring roe clusters into small pieces. Put these ingredients into the storage bag. Add the cuttlefish, carrot, daikon and chili. Pour in the cooled contents of the saucepan. Massage the bag to mix everything well, then close the bag and leave in a cool, dark place for at least 2 hours.

Dried Daikon Pickle Rolls

Many traditional Japanese pickle recipes involve drying daikon. This recipe takes some perseverance but the delicious finished pickle is worth it!

YIELDS: 36 rolls
PREPARATION TIME: 2 hours plus drying time

6 in (15 cm) length daikon radish
4 tablespoons soy sauce
4 tablespoons sake
1½ tablespoons light brown sugar
1 teaspoon mustard powder
2-in (5 cm) piece fresh ginger, peeled and julienned

EQUIPMENT ▸ Flat basket for drying; 2 storage containers, each ¾ cup (180 ml)

AGING ▸ 10 days for sun drying plus 1 day in the refrigerator.

STORAGE ▸ Keeps 2 weeks in the refrigerator

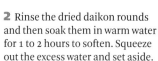

1 Slice the daikon into 36 rounds about $\frac{1}{8}$ in (3 mm) thick. Spread out on a flat basket. Sun dry for 10 days. They should shrivel and harden (left side of the photo). Bring the basket in every night during the drying process.

2 Rinse the dried daikon rounds and then soak them in warm water for 1 to 2 hours to soften. Squeeze out the excess water and set aside.

3 Put the soy sauce, sake and sugar in a saucepan. Bring to a boil, remove from the heat and let cool. This is the pickling solution.

4 Mix the mustard powder in $\frac{1}{2}$ teaspoon of warm water in a cup to form a paste. Set the cup upside down on a plate for about 10 minutes. This will bring out the pungency of the mustard.

5 Spread the daikon rounds out on a flat surface. Spread the mustard on the near half of 18 of the rounds and roll up, away from you. For the remaining 18 rounds, place julienned ginger on the front half of each round and roll up, away from you.

6 Put the mustard rolls into one container with the end flaps facing downward. Put the ginger rolls in the other container in the same way. Pour half of the pickling solution into each container. Put a sheet of plastic wrap directly on top of the rolls in each container. The sheets should be large enough to run up the sides of the containers. Leave in the refrigerator for 1 day.

3-5-8 Yamagata Pickles

The numbers refer to the proportions of salt (3), koji (5) and rice (8) traditionally used to make this pickling medium. This version has less salt. The recipe uses freshly cooked rice that is fermented with koji and water in a rice cooker.

YIELDS: 2 cups (400 g) of pickling medium
PREPARATION TIME: 30 minutes plus time to age pickling medium

Pickling Bed
1½ cups (300 g) cooked Japanese rice
¾ cup (150 g) dried rice koji
⅔ cup (150 ml) water
3 tablespoons kosher or coarse sea salt

Vegetables to Pickle
Carrots
Cucumbers
Turnips

EQUIPMENT ▸ Rice cooker; 1 pint (500 ml) storage container with tight-fitting lid
AGING ▸ 1 day for the pickling bed; 5–6 hours for the vegetables
STORAGE ▸ The pickling bed keeps 3 months in the refrigerator

1 Put the cooked rice, dried rice koji and water in the rice cooker. Mix well.

2 Leave the rice cooker open, but cover it with a cloth. Turn on the rice cooker's "warm" function. Leave on "warm" for 8 hours and then transfer the contents to a mixing bowl.

3 When the rice mixture has cooled to room temperature, add the salt and mix. Transfer to the storage container, seal and set aside. After 12 hours, the pickling medium is done. Refrigerate until ready to use.

4 Add your vegetables of choice to the pickling bed, making sure to submerge them. Cut the vegetables to fit the container. Do not slice them. Set aside for 5 to 6 hours. When removing a vegetable to eat, wipe the pickling medium back into the container with your hands. Cut the vegetables to the desired size. You can use this pickling bed 3 to 4 times within a 3 month period.

Okara Pickles

This Tochigi prefecture favorite uses the soy pulp left over from making tofu, called okara, to make a pickling bed. Use it for almost any vegetable.

YIELDS: 2 cups (400 g) pickling medium
PREPARATION TIME: 10 minutes for the pickling bed

Pickling Medium
1 lb (450 g) fresh okara soy pulp
½ cup (100 g) sugar
1 tablespoon kosher or coarse sea salt
**3 tablespoons white distilled liquor (shochu or vodka),
35% or 70 proof**

Vegetables to Pickle
Carrots
Turnips
Cucumbers

CONTAINER ▸ 1½ quart (1.5 liter) storage container with tight-fitting lid
AGING ▸ 5 days in the refrigerator
STORAGE ▸ Keeps 2 months in the refrigerator

1 Put the okara, sugar, salt and distilled liquor in the storage container. The alcohol retards fermentation and prevents the growth of unwanted microorganisms.

2 Mix the contents of the container well. Store sealed in the refrigerator. The medium is ready to use it at this point.

3 This pickling medium uses relatively little salt, so it's important to rub salt into the vegetables before picking. Use an amount of salt equal to about 1% of the weight of the vegetables. This will also help the vegetables take on the flavor of the okara.

4 Once you put vegetables into the pickling medium, they'll be ready for eating after about 5 days.

"God of Happiness" Pickles

A pickles shop close to Tokyo's Ueno Park invented this pickle. Salt is rubbed into the vegetable, which is then boiled; the pickles are ready to eat soon after preparation.

YIELDS: 12 oz (350 g)
PREPARATION TIME: 1 hour

Small piece daikon radish, about 5 oz (150 g)
Small piece lotus root, about 4 oz (115 g)
1 small carrot
1 Japanese cucumber
Small knob fresh ginger
1 teaspoon kosher or coarse sea salt
⅓ cup (80 ml) soy sauce
⅓ cup (80 ml) mirin
2 tablespoons light brown sugar
1 piece dried kombu seaweed, 2 in (5 cm) square
1 tablespoon rice vinegar
1 tablespoon Soy Cured Shiso Seeds (see page 127), optional

EQUIPMENT ▶ Flat basket for drying; 1 quart (1 liter) resealable plastic bag; 1½ pint (750 ml) storage container
AGING ▶ 12 hours at room temperature
STORAGE ▶ Keeps 2 months in the refrigerator

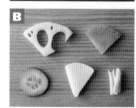

1 Peel the daikon, cut into rounds ½ in (1 cm) thick, then cut the rounds into quarters. Spread the quarters on a flat basket and dry in the sun for about 12 hours (**Photo A**).

2 Quarter the lotus root and the carrot in the same way as the daikon. Rinse the lotus root and let drain. Slice the cucumber thinly. Peel and julienne the ginger (**Photo B**).

3 Put the vegetables, ginger and salt in the plastic bag and mix well. Leave the bag for 1 hour, then remove the vegetables and squeeze out the excess liquid.

4 Put the soy sauce, mirin, brown sugar and kombu in a saucepan and bring to a boil over medium heat. Remove the kombu, then add the vegetables (**Photo C**). When the liquid in the pan returns to a boil, turn off the heat. Remove the vegetables with a slotted spoon, leaving the liquid in the pan. Place the vegetables in the storage container.

5 Return the liquid in the pan to a boil. Turn off the heat, add the vinegar and cool to room temperature.

6 Pour the cooled liquid over the vegetables (**Photo D**). Add the Soy Cured Shiso Seeds if using and leave for 12 hours at room temperature.

Bettara Pickled Daikon with Sweet Sake Mash

This crisp, sweet pickle is traditionally sold at the annual Bettara Pickles Fair in Tokyo. It's made using *amazake*, a sweet low-alcohol rice ferment used for drinking, cooking and preserving. You can find amazake at Asian markets and online, or make it yourself following the recipe below.

YIELDS: about 1 lb (450 g)
PREPARATION TIME: 35 minutes

1 large daikon radish, peeled
Kosher or coarse sea salt (4% of the weight of the peeled daikon)
1¾ cups (400 ml) Amazake Mash (see recipe below)
2 tablespoons sugar
1 dried red chili pepper, deseeded
1 piece dried kombu seaweed, 2 in (5 cm) square

EQUIPMENT ▸ 1 gallon (4 liter) storage bag; metal tray; weights equaling the weight of the daikon
AGING ▸ 1 week in a cool, dry place
STORAGE ▸ Keeps 2 weeks in the refrigerator

1 Peel the daikon and then cut it into three equal lengths. Halve each of these lengths horizontally.

2 Measure out 4% of the weight of the daikon in salt. Salt the daikon pieces evenly. Place them in the storage bag, press out the air, and seal the bag. Put the bag onto a tray.

3 Place a weight equal to the weight of the daikon on top of the daikon. Leave in a cool, dark place for 2 days.

4 Open the bag and discard any liquid that has accumulated. This will help to retain flavor and give you white daikon at the end of the pickling process.

5 Mix the Amazake Mash and sugar and put into the bag with the daikon. Add the red chili pepper and kombu. Shake the bag to mix everything well.

6 Press the air out of the bag, seal and leave in a cool, dark place for 1 week. After about a week, the cut surfaces of the daikon should appear translucent and moist. To eat, cut the daikon into relatively large pieces to enjoy the texture.

Amazake Mash

YIELDS: 1 quart (1 liter)
PREPARATION TIME: About 10 hours

1 cup (180 g) mochi rice, or glutinous rice
1 quart (1 liter) water
1 cup (225 g) rice koji, fresh or dried

1 Rinse the mochi rice and put it into a rice cooker. Add the water and set aside for at least 30 minutes.

2 Cook the rice on "rice porridge" mode to obtain a rice gruel.

3 When cooked, open the lid and let the contents cool to about 140°F (60°C).

4 Crumble the fresh koji, add it to the rice cooker and mix.

5 When the rice loses its stickiness and no longer holds together in clumps, cover the open rice cooker with a cloth. Turn on the rice cooker's "warm" function and leave for at least 8 hours.

6 Taste the amazake mash. If it's sweet, it's done. If it's not sweet enough, keep the rice cooker on "warm" mode for another 2 hours. Amazake mash keeps for 2 weeks in the refrigerator, or 2 months in the freezer.

Dried Salted Mustard Greens

Mustard greens are a staple of wintertime dinner tables in the Nagano region of Japan. These pickles taste great whether young or aged.

YIELDS: 8 oz (225 g)
PREPARATION TIME: 45 minutes plus 3 hours drying time

1 lb (450 g) mustard greens
1 tablespoon kosher or coarse sea salt, 3% weight of the greens
1½ dried red chili peppers, deseeded
1 piece dried kombu seaweed, 2 × 1¼ in (5 × 3 cm)

Brine
½ tablespoon kosher or coarse sea salt
½ cup (125 ml) water

EQUIPMENT ▸ Clothes hangers, cardboard box; 2 heavy-duty plastic bags to fit inside the box; cutting board or other drop lid to fit inside the box; weights totaling 2 lbs (1 kg)
AGING ▸ 5–6 days in a cool, dry place
STORAGE ▸ Keeps 1 month in a cool, dry place

1 Rinse the mustard greens in warm water, taking care to wash away dirt or sand clinging to the stems. Using warm water prevents the stems breaking.

2 Hang the mustard greens on clothes hangers and let them dry for 2 to 3 hours.

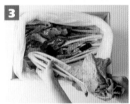

3 Measure out 3% of the weight of the mustard greens in salt. Line the cardboard box with the two plastic bags. Pack half of the greens into the bag and sprinkle on half of the salt.

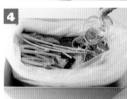

4 Add the remainder of the greens, alternating them so half of the stems are on one side and half on the other side. Sprinkle on the remaining salt, and add the red chili pepper and kombu. Combine the salt and water to make the brine and pour this evenly into the bag.

5 Close the bag and put something flat like a cutting board on top of it. On top of the cutting board, place a weight equal to twice the weight of the greens. Put the box in a cool, dark place. Four days after water has risen in the bag, the mustard greens are ready to eat. Store in a cool, dark place for 1 month.

Marinated Mustard Greens

These sliced pickles have a delightfully crunchy texture.

YIELDS: 1 lb (450 g)
PREPARATION TIME: 35 minutes plus 3 hours drying time

2 lbs (1 kg) mustard greens, top half of the leaves removed (this is the weight after removing the top half of the leaves)
1½ tablespoons kosher or coarse sea salt
½ cup (125 ml) soy sauce
2 tablespoons mirin
2 tablespoons rice vinegar
2 tablespoons light brown sugar
1 dried red chili pepper, seeded
1 piece dried kombu seaweed, 2 in (5 cm) square

EQUIPMENT ▸ 1 gallon (4 liter) resealable storage bag; weights totaling 4 lb (2 kg)
AGING ▸ 12 hours in the refrigerator
STORAGE ▸ Keeps 1 week in the refrigerator

1 Wash the greens in warm water. Cut into 1 in (2.5 cm) lengths and put in the storage bag. Sprinkle on the salt and seal. Place the weight on the bag. Leave in a cool, dark place for 1 hour.

2 Put the soy sauce, mirin, vinegar, brown sugar, red chili pepper and kombu in a saucepan over medium heat. Bring to a boil, remove from the heat and cool to room temperature. Set aside.

3 Drain the greens in a colander and discard the liquid. Squeeze additional water from the greens. Return the greens to the bag and pour in the cooled contents of the pan. Refrigerate for 12 hours.

Dried Salted Mustard Greens

Kyoto Pickle Medley

Called *shibazuke* in Japanese, these are one of the most popular souvenirs from Kyoto. They get their characteristic color and tartness from red plum vinegar and their aroma from shiso leaves.

YIELDS: 8 oz (225 g)
PREPARATION TIME: 35 minutes

3 myoga ginger buds
5 oz (150 g) slender Asian eggplant
3 Japanese cucumbers, about 11 oz (300 g)
Small piece fresh ginger
5 green shiso leaves
Kosher or coarse sea salt (1% of the total weight of the
    above vegetables)
1 tablespoon mirin
1 tablespoon light brown sugar
4 tablespoons red plum vinegar

> **NOTE** The vegetables should have a combined weight of about 1 lb (450 g).

EQUIPMENT ▸ 1 quart (1 liter) resealable storage bag; weights totaling 2 lb (1 kg)
AGING ▸ 3 days in a cool, dark place
STORAGE ▸ Keeps 1 week in the refrigerator

1 Halve each myoga bud so you have 6 equally sized pieces. Halve the eggplant and cut into slices ¼ in (5 mm) thick. Rinse in water and drain. Do the same with the cucumber, but make the slices ⅛ in (3 mm) thick. Peel the ginger and julienne. Cut the shiso leaves into ¼ in (5 mm) squares.

2 Put all the vegetables, except the shiso, in the storage bag. Add the salt. Add the mirin and the sugar and mix the contents of the bag. Close the bag and put the weight on top of it. Leave in a cool, dark place for 3 to 4 hours.

3 Open the bag and squeeze as much liquid as you can from the vegetables. Add the red plum vinegar and shiso leaves to the bag, close it, and put the weight back on top of it.

4 Leave for an additional 2 to 3 days. The pickles are ready to eat when the vegetables have taken on a red hue.

Fish Sauce Pickles

In this Kyoto favorite, sake and fish sauce work together to produce a mildly flavored pickle. Traditionally, Ishiru fish sauce from the Noto Peninsula on the Sea of Japan coast is used in this recipe, but you can use any kind of fish sauce available.

YIELDS: 8 oz (225 g)
PREPARATION TIME: 25 minutes

1 Japanese cucumber, about 4 oz (115 g)
1 piece daikon radish, about 8 oz (225 g)
1 large carrot, about 4 oz (115 g)
4 tablespoons sake
2 tablespoons fish sauce
1 piece dried kombu seaweed, 2 in (5 cm) square
1 dried red chili pepper

A

B

C

1 Cut the cucumber into 2-in (5 cm) lengths, then quarter each of these lengths. Peel the daikon and carrot and cut them into lengths about the same size as the cucumbers.

2 Put the sake in a saucepan, bring to a boil and then turn off the heat. Add the fish sauce (**photo A**).

3 Place the cucumbers, daikon and carrots in the storage bag and add the kombu and red chili pepper. Add the liquid from the pan while it is still warm (**photo B**).

4 Shake the bag to mix everything well and then put the bag into the refrigerator for at least 3 hours (**photo C**).

CONTAINER ▸ 1 gallon (4 liter) resealable storage bag
AGING ▸ 3 hours in the refrigerator
STORAGE ▸ Keeps 3 days in the refrigerator

Takana Pickles

Takana is a pungent variety of Japanese mustard greens and this pickle is popular in Kumamoto prefecture in Kyushu. Use regular mustard greens if you can't get hold of takana.

YIELDS: 1 lb (450 g)
PREPARATION TIME: 50 minutes

2 lbs (1 kg) mustard greens
2 tablespoons kosher or coarse sea salt (3% of the weight of the mustard greens)
2 dried red chili peppers, deseeded
1 piece dried kombu seaweed, 2 × 4 in (5 × 10 cm)

EQUIPMENT ▸ Metal tray; 7 quart (7 liter) enamel container; heavy-duty plastic bag to fit inside the container; weights totaling 4 lb (2 kg); small, resealable storage bags for small portions
AGING ▸ Keep in a cool, dark place for 2 days to 2 weeks
STORAGE ▸ Keeps 2 weeks in the refrigerator

1 Rinse the greens vigorously in water, making sure to remove any dirt or sand between the stems at the base. Hang the greens on clothes hangers and dry them in the sun for 2 to 3 days.

2 Weigh the greens and measure out 3% of that weight in salt. Take each bunch of greens and spread open on a cutting board. Sprinkle with salt all over, especially the stems.

3 Use your hands to massage each bunch. This is to soften the greens and make them easier to pack.

4 Squeeze as much liquid as you can out of the greens, working over a metal tray. Reserve this liquid.

5 Put a plastic bag into the bottom of the enamel container and open the bag up. Pack the greens into the bag as tightly as possible.

6 Add any of the liquid that collected in the tray in step 4. Put the red chili pepper and kombu on top of the greens, press all the air out of the bag and seal.

7 Put a weight equal to twice the weight of the greens on top of the bag. Keep the container in a cool, dark place for 2 days. After two days, open the bag, divide the greens into small portions and place in storage bags, adding a bit of the liquid to each bag. Store bags in the refrigerator. If you would like to thoroughly age your greens, keep the container in a cool, dark place for 2 weeks, before transferring the greens to storage bags.

Pickled Turnips

Kyoto's traditional *senmai-zuke* pickles are traditionally made with the local *shogoin* turnip. But these pickles are just as delicious made with regular white or red turnip.

YIELDS: 1 lb (450 g)
PREPARATION TIME: 30 minutes

2 lbs (1 kg) turnip, red or white
1½ tablespoons kosher or coarse sea salt (2% of the weight of the turnips)
½ cup (100 g) sugar (10% of the weight of the turnips)
¾ cup (180 ml) rice vinegar (20% of the weight of the turnips)
1 piece dried kombu seaweed, 2 in (5 cm) square
1 dried red chili pepper, deseeded

EQUIPMENT ▶ Metal tray; plastic wrap; weights totaling 2 lb (1 kg); 1 gallon (4 liter) resealable storage bag
AGING ▶ 4–5 hours in a cool, dark place, then 1 day in the refrigerator
STORAGE ▶ Keeps 2 weeks in the refrigerator

1 Peel the turnip and slice into thin rounds.

2 Lay the turnip slices in the metal tray, so that they overlap one another. Sprinkle salt on each slice as you do this. When you finish, press a sheet of plastic wrap down onto the turnips to seal out air. The wrap should be large enough to run up the sides of the metal tray.

3 Put the weight on top of the turnips and then put the tray in a cool, dark place for 4 to 5 hours.

4 Put the sugar and vinegar in a saucepan over low heat. When the sugar has dissolved, remove from the heat.

5 After 4 to 5 hours, water will have accumulated in the metal tray. Remove the turnip slices and let them drain. Transfer them to the storage bag and add the sweetened vinegar, kombu and chili pepper. Seal the bag and put it into the refrigerator for at least 1 day.

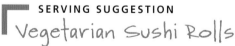

SERVING SUGGESTION
Vegetarian Sushi Rolls

Make a dressing of 3 parts rice vinegar and 1 part sugar and add to cooked short grain white rice to make sushi rice. Form the sushi rice into bite-size oblong dumpling shapes. Wrap each in half of a slice of pickled turnip. Secure the roll with a boiled sprig of *mitsuba* parsley or regular parsley and garnish with a bit of julienned yuzu zest.

Pickling with Grapes

I'd like to end this section on regional favorites with a couple of recipes I grew up with in rural Japan. I come from a family that has been farming for eight generations in Tochigi, a mountainous prefecture north of Tokyo. Grapes and rice are the main products, but the farm also turns out various types of vegetable. Spring, summer, fall and winter, our dinner table was never without pickles made by my mother and grandmother from plums, daikon radish, cucumbers, shiso seeds, Napa cabbage and any number of other vegetables. "Machiko, bring some pickled cabbage to the kitchen please." That was my cue to head to the corner of our garden where we kept a shed just for pickles. Inside was crammed with barrels, crocks and jars of pickles, as well as jams, all arranged in neat lines. My own pickle-making experience dates back to that time in my life. Among the many recipes I learned from my grandmother and mother, it's the grape-pickled daikon that reminds me most of home. Try it and you'll be surprised at how delicious the combination of daikon and grapes can be!

Pickled Daikon and Grapes

Red Grape Pickled Daikon

Red Grape Pickled Daikon

Japanese Kyoho grapes give this pickle its beautiful purple color. Concord grapes are similar in size and flavor.

YIELDS: 12 oz (300 g)
PREPARATION TIME: 30 minutes

½ daikon radish, about 1 lb (450 g)
1 teaspoon kosher or coarse sea salt
1 bunch red grapes, about 1 lb (450 g)
5 tablespoons sugar
2 tablespoons kosher or coarse sea salt
3 tablespoons white wine vinegar

CONTAINER ▸ 1 gallon (4 liter) resealable storage bag
AGING ▸ 2 days in the refrigerator
STORAGE ▸ Keeps 2 weeks in the refrigerator

1 Peel the daikon and cut into 4 quarters, lengthwise. Put the pieces into the storage bag, sprinkle on the 1 teaspoon of salt, seal the bag and leave for about 30 minutes.

2 Separate the grapes from the bunch, rinse them in water and drain. Put the grapes into a saucepan and add the sugar and the 2 tablespoons of salt and mash the grapes well. Place the saucepan over medium heat.

3 Stir with a spatula. As the grapes simmer, they will become rich in color and the contents of the pan will thicken. When the liquid becomes slow to cover the bottom of the pan as you drag the spatula over it, turn the heat off and let cool. Mix in the white wine vinegar.

4 Remove the daikon pieces from the bag used in step 1. Let them drain and then put them into a new bag. Add the simmered grapes to the bag. Massage the bag to ensure the daikon is evenly exposed to the grapes. Seal the bag and leave in the refrigerator for 2 days.

Pickled Daikon and Grapes

Using fresh, uncooked grapes means there will be live yeast in the pickling process. Tartness will intensify as time passes, so this pickle is best consumed in short order!

YIELDS: 10 oz (280 g)
PREPARATION TIME: 20 minutes

1 piece daikon radish, about 8 oz (225 g)
1 bunch Muscat grapes, about 5 oz (150 g)
2 tablespoons sugar
1 tablespoon kosher or coarse sea salt
1½ teaspoon rice vinegar

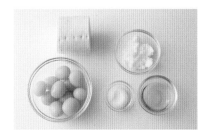

CONTAINER ▸ 1 quart (1 liter) reseable storage bag
AGING ▸ 12 hours in the refrigerator
STORAGE ▸ Keeps 1 week in the refrigerator

1 Peel the daikon and cut into quarters.

2 Cut the grapes in half and remove any seeds.

3 Put the daikon halves, grapes and the rest of the ingredients into the storage bag. Lightly massage the bag to mix the contents and then leave the bag in the refrigerator for at least 12 hours.

Chapter 3

Instant Pickles

Instant pickles are just the thing for those times when you want to add something to the menu, or maybe you feel like a meal needs more vegetables. All the delicious recipes in this section are easy to make and most are ready to eat in a day or less. In addition to being quick to make, these recipes also keep well, so they can be a regular presence in your refrigerator.

Salted Cabbage Pickle

Speed up the salting process by leaving a little air in the bag and shaking it. Doing this can give you a pickle ready to eat in as little as 1 hour.

YIELDS: 8 oz (225 g)
PREPARATION TIME: 20 minutes

½ green cabbage, about 1 lb (450 g)
2 teaspoons kosher or coarse sea salt (2.5% of the weight of the cabbage)
Handful julienned dried kombu seaweed
1 tablespoon rice vinegar

CONTAINER ▸ 1 quart (1 liter) resealable storage bag
AGING ▸ 1 hour in the refrigerator
STORAGE ▸ Keeps 3 days in the refrigerator

1 Remove the cabbage core and discard. Roughly chop the cabbage. Put the chopped cabbage into the storage bag and with the rest of the ingredients (**photo A**).

2 Let some air into the bag, close the bag and shake it (**photo B**) to mix the contents well.

3 Remove the air from the bag. Seal and put into the refrigerator for 1 hour

Sesame Cabbage Pickle

Preparing this pickle in a bag makes it possible to speed the pickling process with a little manual encouragement. Sesame oil boosts the aroma and the depth of flavor.

YIELDS: 8 oz (225 g)
PREPARATION TIME: 25 minutes

½ green cabbage, about 1 lb (450 g)
Heaping teaspoon kosher or coarse sea salt (2% of the weight of the cabbage)
1 tablespoon roasted white sesame seeds
1 tablespoon sesame oil
⅓ teaspoon kosher or coarse sea salt (0.5% of the weight of the cabbage)

CONTAINER ▸ 1 quart (1 liter) resealable storage bag
AGING ▸ None
STORAGE ▸ Keeps 3 days in the refrigerator

1 Remove the cabbage core and discard. Roughly chop the cabbage.

2 Put the chopped cabbage into the storage bag and add the heaping teaspoon of salt. Close the bag with some air inside and shake it to ensure the cabbage is evenly salted (**photo A**).

3 Knead the cabbage through the bag until it softens, then drain off any liquid.

4 Add the remaining ingredients to the bag. After lightly massaging the bag to mix the contents (**Photo B**), the cabbage is ready to eat.

Umami Cabbage

Simply soak roughly cut and brined cabbage in umami vinegar soy sauce for a short time and cut it into bite-size pieces when you're ready to eat.

YIELDS: 1 lb (450 g)
PREPARATION TIME: 3 hours

1 green cabbage, about 1¾ lbs (800 g)
2 teaspoons kosher or coarse sea salt (about 1.5% of the weight of the cabbage)
1 piece dried kombu seaweed, 2 in (5 cm) square
1¾ cups (400 ml) water
5 tablespoons rice vinegar
2 tablespoons light soy sauce
3 tablespoons sugar
1 teaspoon kosher or coarse sea salt

EQUIPMENT ▸ 1 gallon (4 liter) resealable storage bag; metal tray; weights totaling 3½–4 lbs (1.5–2 kg)
AGING ▸ 2–3 hours in a cool, dark place, then 12 hours in the refrigerator
STORAGE ▸ Keeps 3 days in the refrigerator

1 Split the cabbage into four equal pieces. Remove and discard the core. Sprinkle the 2 teaspoons of salt evenly over the cut surfaces of the cabbage.

2 Put the cabbage quarters into the storage bag. Press the air out of the bag and seal it. Put the bag into the metal tray and put the weight on top of the bag. Keep the tray in a cool, dark place for 2 to 3 hours.

3 After 2 to 3 hours, open the bag and dump out the water that will have accumulated. This brining process prevents the pickles from becoming too mushy.

4 Add the rest of the ingredients to the bag. Massage the bag to mix the contents well. Put the bag into the refrigerator for 12 hours.

Broccoli Rabe in Seasoned Kombu

Wrapping kombu around a vegetable will increase its umami and produce deeper flavor in the resulting pickle. This recipe can be made with *nanohana*, the young shoots of the rapeseed plant, as pictured, or with broccoli rabe.

YIELDS: 12 oz (350 g)
PREPARATION TIME: 30 minutes

5 tablespoons sake
1 large sheet dried kombu seaweed,
   12–16 in (30–40 cm) sq
1 lb (450 g) young broccoli rabe
Pinch of salt
½ teaspoon kosher or coarse sea salt

EQUIPMENT ▸ Brush; flat basket for cooling; plastic wrap
AGING ▸ 12 hours in the refrigerator
STORAGE ▸ Keeps 1 week in the refrigerator

1 In a small saucepan on medium heat bring the sake to a boil. Reduce the heat and simmer for 1 minute so that the alcohol cooks off. Remove the pan from the heat. Use a brush to coat and moisten the kombu with the sake.

2 Trim off the bottoms of the broccoli rabe stems. Bring a pan of water to a boil, then put in the broccoli rabe with the pinch of salt. When the water comes back to a boil, wait 30 seconds, remove the broccoli rabe stems and then lay them out on a flat basket to cool.

3 Cut off enough of the broccoli rabe stems to make each sprig as long as the kombu is wide. Place the broccoli rabe sprigs side by side all along the length of the kombu. Sprinkle on the ½ teaspoon of salt. Roll up the kombu with the broccoli rabe inside.

4 Enclose the roll in a sheet of plastic wrap and place the roll in the refrigerator for 12 hours.

Asparagus in Seasoned Kombu

Kombu-wrapped vegetables are a perfect little something to go with drinks.

YIELDS: 12 oz (350 g)
PREPARATION TIME: 30 minutes

5 tablespoons sake
1 large sheet dried kombu seaweed,
    12–16 in (30–40 cm) sq
12 green asparagus spears, about
    1 lb (450 g)
Pinch of salt
½ teaspoon kosher or coarse sea salt

EQUIPMENT ▸ Brush; flat basket for cooling; plastic wrap
AGING ▸ 12 hours in the refrigerator
STORAGE ▸ Keeps 1 week in the refrigerator

1 In a small saucepan on medium heat bring the sake to a boil. Reduce the heat and simmer for 1 minute so that the alcohol cooks off. Remove the pan from heat. Use a brush to coat and moisten the kombu with the sake.

2 Peel the ends of the asparagus (**photo A**) and remove all of the triangular leaves.

3 Bring a pan of water to a boil and put in the asparagus with the pinch of salt (**photo B**). When the water comes back to a boil remove the asparagus and then lay on a flat basket to cool. When cool, cut the asparagus into even lengths, as shown in the large photo above.

4 Place the asparagus pieces side by side along the length of the kombu. Sprinkle on the ½ teaspoon of salt. Roll up the kombu with the asparagus pieces inside. Enclose the roll in a sheet of plastic wrap and place in the refrigerator for 12 hours.

Quick Spicy Pickles

These pickles are often made with udo, a traditional Japanese vegetable, called spikenard or aralia cordata in English. Asparagus is a great substitute if you can't get hold of udo.

YIELDS: 2 cups (500 ml)
PREPARATION TIME: 25 minutes

1 udo, about 5 oz (150 g), or 10 medium asparagus spears
Dash of rice vinegar

Pickling Solution
½ cup (125 ml) rice vinegar
½ cup (125 ml) white wine
½ cup (125 ml) water
4 tablespoons sugar
2 teaspoons kosher or coarse sea salt
1 bay leaf
1 dried red chili pepper, deseeded
1 teaspoon black peppercorns

CONTAINER ▶ 1 pint (500 ml) heat-resistant storage jar
AGING ▶ 1 day in a cool, dark place
STORAGE ▶ Keeps 2 weeks in a cool, dark place

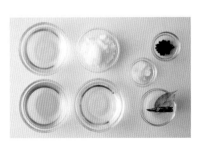

1 If using udo, cut into 2-in (5-cm) lengths and peel, taking off a bit of the underlying flesh in the process. Cut the pieces into thin rectangles, as shown in the picture. Soak the udo pieces in water with a dash of rice vinegar for about 10 minutes (**photo A**). Drain the udo and put it into the storage jar.

2 If using asparagus, bring a pan of lightly salted water to a boil, then put in the asparagus. When the water comes back to a boil, wait for 30 seconds, drain and cool. Cut into 2-in (5-cm) lengths and put into the storage jar.

3 Bring the pickling solution ingredients to a boil in a saucepan (**photo B**).

4 While the pickling solution is still hot, pour it into the storage jar (**photo C**). Keep the jar in a cool, dark place for at least 1 day.

Asparagus and Broccoli Rabe in Sake Lees

Sake lees, called *sake kasu* in Japanese, is a by-product of making sake and can be bought at Japanese groceries in paste form. Its high nutritional value makes it a popular pickling medium.

YIELDS: 12 oz (350 g)
PREPARATION TIME: 45 minutes

5 green asparagus spears
Bunch young broccoli rabe,
  about 5 oz (150 g)
Pinch of salt

EQUIPMENT ▸ Flat basket; plastic wrap
AGING ▸ 1 day in the refrigerator
STORAGE ▸ Keeps 1 week in the refrigerator

Pickling Medium
¾ cup (225 g) sake lees
  paste
2½ tablespoons miso
4 tablespoons sugar
⅓ cup (80 ml) sake
½ teaspoon kosher or
  coarse sea salt

SAKE LEES PICKLING BED
You can use the above ingredients to make a sake lees pickling bed. It keeps 2 months covered and refrigerated. Use it to pickle celery, bell peppers, even fresh squid and other fish.

1 Puree the pickling medium ingredients in a food processor.

2 Peel the bottom halves of the asparagus spears and remove the triangular leaves.

3 Blanch the asparagus and broccoli rabe with a pinch of salt. Lay the vegetables on a flat basket to cool. Cut the asparagus into four equal lengths.

4 Spread 2 sheets of plastic wrap on a flat surface. On each, spread half the sake lees paste in a thin layer. Lay the asparagus spears side by side in the middle of one of the pieces of plastic wrap. Do the same for the broccoli rabe. Fold the left and right sides of the wrap onto the top of the vegetables to enclose vegetables in sake lees paste. Put the wrapped vegetables into the refrigerator for 1 day.

Miso Cured Burdock and Carrot Batons

Fresh burdock root has a texture similar to carrot and a taste similar to artichoke. You can find it in the produce section of Asian markets and many health-food stores.

YIELDS: approx 16 pieces
PREPARATION TIME: 30 minutes

1 burdock root
Dash of rice vinegar
2 medium carrots
¾ cup (200 g) miso
8 tablespoons sugar
2 teaspoons rice vinegar

EQUIPMENT ▶ 1½ quart (1.5 liter) storage container; plastic wrap
AGING ▶ 12 hours in the refrigerator
STORAGE ▶ Keeps 2 weeks in the refrigerator

1 Scrape the surface of the burdock root and then cut the root into 4 in (10 cm) batons. Halve each length vertically and soak in water with the dash of vinegar. Peel the carrots and cut into 4 in (10 cm) batons.

2 Drain the burdock root and put into boiling water for about 3 minutes (**photo A**) and then drain in a sieve.

3 Put the miso, sugar and 2 teaspoons of rice vinegar into a bowl and mix. Spread half of this mixture over the bottom of the storage container. Arrange the carrot and burdock root pieces in neat rows in the container. Spread the remainder of the miso-sugar-vinegar mixture on top of the carrot and burdock root pieces (**photo B**).

4 Press a piece of plastic wrap onto the carrot and burdock root pieces (**photo C**). The piece of wrap should be large enough to run up the sides of the container. Put the container into the refrigerator for 12 hours.

Burdock and Shiso Pickles

Fresh burdock root is a common ingredient in Japan. Parboiling results in pickles that have a satisfying firmness.

YIELDS: approx 20 pieces
PREPARATION TIME: 45 minutes

2 burdock roots
Dash of rice vinegar
1 tablespoon soy sauce
20 large green shiso leaves

Pickling Solution
½ cup (125 ml) soy sauce
½ cup (125 ml) mirin
4 tablespoons sugar
1 dried red chili pepper, deseeded

EQUIPMENT ▶ Metal tray; plastic wrap
AGING ▶ 1 hour in a cool, dark place
STORAGE ▶ Keeps 1 week in the refrigerator

1 Scrape the surface of the burdock root and cut it into 3 in (8 cm) lengths. Soak in water with the dash of rice vinegar. Drain the burdock root, put into boiling water for about 3 minutes and then drain in a sieve.

2 Transfer the burdock root to a mixing bowl. Add the soy sauce while the burdock root is still hot and mix well.

3 Dip the shiso leaves in boiling water, immediately dunk them in cold water and then let them drain. Spread a leaf out, with the base of the leaf nearest to you. Lay a piece of burdock root across the base of the leaf and then roll up the leaf. Repeat for all of the burdock root pieces. Arrange all the wrapped burdock root pieces in neat rows in the metal tray.

4 Put the pickling solution ingredients in a saucepan, bring to a boil, then remove from the heat. When cool, pour evenly into the metal tray.

5 Press a piece of plastic wrap over the burdock. The wrap should be large enough to run up the sides of the tray. Put the tray into the refrigerator for at least 1 hour.

Wasabi Greens Pickled in Sake Lees

Spicy wasabi greens make a pungent pickle. Watercress can be substituted although the texture may be different.

YIELDS: 6 oz (170 g)
PREPARATION TIME: 30 minutes

12 oz (350 g) wasabi greens
½ tablespoon kosher or coarse sea salt
¾ cup (225 g) sake lees paste
2 tablespoons mirin
2 tablespoons miso
¼ teaspoon kosher or coarse sea salt

EQUIPMENT ▸ 1 quart (1 liter) resealable storage bag;
    1 pint (500 ml) storage container
AGING ▸ 1 day in the refrigerator
STORAGE ▸ Keeps 1 month in the refrigerator

1 Trim off the ends of the stems of the wasabi greens. Cut the stems and the leaves into 1½ in (4 cm) lengths.

2 Put the stems and leaves into a mixing bowl and sprinkle with the salt. Use your hands to massage the greens until they soften. This will break down cell walls and bring out the pungency of the greens.

3 Prepare a bowl of ice water. Heat a saucepan of water until you can see tiny bubbles forming on the bottom of the pan. Put the wasabi greens into the saucepan for 10 seconds and then transfer them to the bowl of ice water.

4 Squeeze the water out of the greens and put them in the storage bag. Let a little air into the bag, hold it closed and shake it. This will improve the flavor. Expel the air from the bag, seal and refrigerate for 1 hour.

5 Put all the other ingredients in a mixing bowl and mix well. Transfer the resulting paste to the storage container, add the wasabi greens and mix well. Cover the container and leave in the refrigerator for at least 1 day.

Sweet Pickled Wasabi Greens

These sweet pickles are quick, easy and satisfying.

YIELDS: 6 oz (170 g)
PREPARATION TIME: 30 mins

12 oz (350 g) wasabi greens
½ tablespoon kosher or coarse sea salt

Pickling Solution
4 tablespoons rice vinegar
4½ tablespoons sugar
½ tablespoon light soy sauce
1 teaspoon kosher or coarse sea salt

EQUIPMENT ▸ 1 quart (1 liter) resealable storage bag;
    1 pint (500 ml) storage jar
AGING ▸ 1 hour in a cool, dark place
STORAGE ▸ Keeps 1 month in the refrigerator

1 Follow steps 1–4 for Wasabi Greens Pickled in Sake Lees (left).

2 Put the pickling solution ingredients in the storage jar, close the jar and shake it to mix. Open the jar and add the wasabi greens. Close the jar and shake to mix again. Place the jar in the refrigerator for at least 1 hour.

Wasabi Greens with Soy Sauce

The faint sweetness of the pickling solution partners superbly with the pungency of wasabi greens.

YIELDS: 6 oz (170 g)
PREPARATION TIME: 25 mins

12 oz (350 g) wasabi greens
½ tablespoon kosher or coarse sea salt
½ cup (125 ml) soy sauce
4 tablespoons mirin

EQUIPMENT ▸ 1 quart (1 liter) resealable storage bag;
    1 pint (500 ml) storage jar
AGING ▸ 1 hour in a cool, dark place
STORAGE ▸ Keeps 1 month in the refrigerator

1 Follow steps 1–4 for Wasabi Greens Pickled in Sake Lees (left).

2 Put the soy sauce and mirin into a saucepan, bring to a boil, then remove the pan from the heat and allow to cool.

3 Put the wasabi greens into the storage jar and pour in the cooled contents of the saucepan. Put the jar in the refrigerator for at least 1 hour.

Sweet Pickled Wasabi Greens

Wasabi Greens with
Soy Sauce

Wasabi Greens Pickled in
Sake Lees

Celery Pickled in Lemon Oil

Lemon oil—a combination of lemon zest, lemon juice and salt—has become a popular seasoning in Japan. Combine it with celery for a truly sublime flavor experience.

YIELDS: 4 oz (115 g)
PREPARATION TIME: 20 minutes

2 stalks celery
½ organic lemon
1 teaspoon kosher or coarse sea salt
½ cup (125 ml) olive oil

CONTAINER ▸ 1 pint (500 ml) airtight storage jar
AGING ▸ 12 hours in a cool, dark place
STORAGE ▸ Keeps 1 month in the refrigerator

1 Remove the strings from the celery and cut the stalks into 1 in (2.5 cm) lengths. Bring a pan of lightly salted water to a boil and put in the celery. When the water comes back to a boil, wait 30 seconds and drain in a sieve.

2 Peel and julienne the lemon zest. Juice the lemon.

3 Put the celery in the storage jar. Put the lemon zest, lemon juice, salt and olive oil in a bowl, mix and add to the storage jar. Leave in a cool, dark place for 12 hours.

Celery Pickled in Fish Sauce

This Thai-flavored pickle is a fusion of saltiness, umami, spiciness and sweetness.

YIELDS: 4 oz (115 g)
PREPARATION TIME: 20 minutes

2 stalks celery
1½ tablespoons fish sauce
1 tablespoon sugar
1 tablespoon lemon juice
1 dried red chili pepper, sliced into rings
1 garlic clove, thinly sliced

CONTAINER ▸ 1 quart (1 liter) resealable storage bag
AGING ▸ 30 minutes in the refrigerator
STORAGE ▸ Keeps 1 week in the refrigerator

1 Remove the strings from the celery and cut the stalks into 2 in (5 cm) lengths. Bring a pan of lightly salted water to a boil and put in the celery. When the water comes back to a boil, wait 30 seconds and drain in a sieve (see photo).

2 Put the celery into the storage bag. Put all the other ingredients in a bowl, mix and pour into the storage bag. Massage the bag then put into the refrigerator for about 30 minutes.

Honey Miso Pickled Celery

These pickles are at their best when freshly made.

YIELDS: 4 oz (115 g)
PREPARATION TIME: 15 minutes plus 1 hour in the refrigerator

2 stalks celery
½ teaspoon kosher or coarse sea salt
3 tablespoons miso
1 tablespoon honey
Small handful raisins

CONTAINER ▸ 1 quart (1 liter) storage bag
AGING ▸ 30 minutes in the refrigerator
STORAGE ▸ Keeps 1 week refrigerated

1 Remove the strings from the celery and cut the stalks into bite-size pieces.

2 Place the celery into the storage bag, add the salt and massage the bag. Put the bag into the refrigerator for about 1 hour. Remove the bag from the refrigerator and drain the water that has accumulated.

3 Put the honey and miso in a bowl and mix well. Transfer this mixture to the storage bag and add the raisins. Seal the bag and put it into the refrigerator for about 30 minutes.

Sweet & Sour Onions

A sweet onion variety, such as Vidalia, works well for this recipe.

YIELDS: 8 oz (225 g)
PREPARATION TIME: 20 minutes

1 dried red chili pepper, deseeded and sliced into rings
⅓ cup (80 ml) soy sauce
4 tablespoons light brown sugar
4 tablespoons rice vinegar
2 onions, about 1 lb (450 g)

EQUIPMENT ▸ 1½ quart (1.5 liter) storage container; plastic wrap
AGING ▸ 12 hours in the refrigerator
STORAGE ▸ Keeps 1 week in the refrigerator

1 Put the chili pepper, soy sauce, sugar and vinegar into a saucepan. Bring the pan to a boil, remove from the heat and let cool.

2 Cut the onions into thin wedges and put into the storage container. Pour in the cooled contents of the pan.

3 Place a sheet of plastic wrap directly on the onions. It should be large enough to run up the sides of the container. Refrigerate for 12 hours. After 3 to 4 hours, the level liquid in the container will have risen to the top of the onions.

Crunchy Cucumber Pickles

Cucumber Mustard Pickles

Salt and sugar are the keys for infusing flavor.

YIELDS: 10 oz (280 g)
PREPARATION TIME: 10 minutes

4 Japanese cucumbers, about 1 lb (450 g)
1 tablespoon kosher or coarse sea salt (3% of the weight of the cucumbers)
3 tablespoons sugar (10% of the weight of the cucumbers)
2 teaspoons yellow mustard powder (1% of the weight of the cucumbers)

CONTAINER ▸ 1 quart (1 liter) resealable storage bag
AGING ▸ 2 days in the refrigerator
STORAGE ▸ Keeps 1 week in the refrigerator

1 Trim off both ends of the cucumbers and cut the cucumbers in half. Put the cucumber halves into the storage bag and add the salt, sugar and mustard powder.

2 Gently massage the bag to mix the contents well. Leave in the refrigerator for 2 days.

Crunchy Cucumber Pickles

After boiling and cooling in the pickling solution, this pickle is ready to eat.

YIELDS: 10 oz (280 g)
PREPARATION TIME: 20 minutes

4 Japanese cucumbers, about 1 lb (450 g)
3 in (8 cm) piece fresh ginger
½ cup (125 ml) soy sauce
8 tablespoons mirin
2 tablespoons rice vinegar

EQUIPMENT ▸ None
AGING ▸ None
STORAGE ▸ Keeps 2 weeks refrigerated

Cucumber Yogurt Pickles

These are a great side dish for a curry.

YIELDS: 10 oz (280 g)
PREPARATION TIME: 10 minutes

4 Japanese cucumbers, about 1 lb (450 g)
1½ tablespoons kosher or coarse sea salt (5% of the weight of the cucumbers)
1¼ cups (300 g) plain yogurt

CONTAINER ▸ 1 quart (1 liter) storage bag
AGING ▸ 12 hours in the refrigerator
STORAGE ▸ Keeps 5 days refrigerated

1 Cut the cucumbers into rounds 1 in (2.5 cm) thick. Julienne the ginger.

2 Put the soy sauce, mirin and vinegar in a saucepan and bring to a boil over high heat. Add the cucumber and ginger, and stir (**photo A**). Remove from the heat.

3 When the pan has cooled, bring back to a boil over high heat, then remove from the heat. Repeat this process one more time (**photo B**). When cool, the pickles are ready.

1 Trim off both ends of the cucumbers and cut the cucumbers in half. Put the cucumber halves into the storage bag and add the salt. Gently massage the bag to evenly coat the cucumber halves with salt.

2 Add the yogurt to the bag. Massage the bag to coat the cucumber with yogurt. Leave in the refrigerator for 12 hours.

Cucumber Mustard Pickles

Cucumber Yogurt Pickles

Chayote Pickles with Kombu and Shiso

The kombu seaweed provides umami, and the shiso and ginger lend a fragrant aroma.

YIELDS: 8 oz (225 g)
PREPARATION TIME: 25 minutes

1 lb (450 g) chayote
2 teaspoons kosher or coarse sea salt
6 green shiso leaves
Small piece fresh ginger

Pickling Solution
Handful julienned dried kombu seaweed
1 dried red chili pepper, deseeded and sliced into rings
1 teaspoon light soy sauce

CONTAINER ▸ 1 quart (1 liter) resealable storage bag
AGING ▸ 30 minutes in the refrigerator
STORAGE ▸ Keeps 5 days in the refrigerator

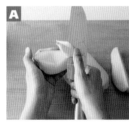

1 Quarter the chayote and remove the core (**photo A**). Cut each quarter into ¼ in (5 mm) pieces. If you're working with a large chayote, peeling it will make it easier to eat. See instructions on the facing page.

2 Sprinkle the chayote with the salt, set aside for 30 minutes, then squeeze out the water.

3 Julienne the shiso leaves. Peel and julienne the ginger.

4 Put the chayote, shiso, ginger and the pickling solution ingredients in the storage bag (**photo B**). Massage the bag and then leave in the refrigerator for 30 minutes.

CHAYOTE
Chayote is a variety of squash with a crunchy texture and can be either green or white. It doesn't have much flavor of its own but is great for pickles as it absorbs other flavors and has a satisfying crunch. It's widely available in supermarkets.

Cucumber Pick-Me-Up Pickles

With garlic to stimulate the appetite even on a hot day, this pickle is ideal for summer. It's also ready to eat in no time!

YIELDS: 8 oz (225 g)
PREPARATION TIME: 25 minutes

CONTAINER ▶ 1 quart (1 liter) resealable storage bag
AGING ▶ 1 hour in a cool, dark place
STORAGE ▶ Keeps 5 days in the refrigerator

3 Japanese cucumbers, about 12 oz (350 g)
1 dried red chili pepper, deseeded
3 tablespoons light soy sauce
2 tablespoons mirin
½ teaspoon grated garlic
1 tablespoon sesame oil
1 tablespoon ground white sesame seeds

1 Halve the cucumbers and then cut each of the halves into 1½ in (4 cm) lengths. Break the red chili pepper into 2 to 4 pieces.

2 Put the cucumber and chili pepper into the storage bag. Add the rest of the ingredients and massage the bag. Leave the bag in the refrigerator for 1 hour.

Cucumber Pick-Me-Up Pickles

Spicy Chayote Pickles

Parboiling in a pickling solution with red chili pepper infuses flavor and pungency.

YIELDS: 6 oz (170 g)
PREPARATION TIME: 25 minutes

EQUIPMENT ▶ 1 quart (1 liter) airtight storage jar
AGING ▶ None
STORAGE ▶ Keeps 2 weeks in the refrigerator

12 oz (350 g) chayote
½ cup (125 ml) soy sauce
4 tablespoons mirin
2 tablespoons rice vinegar
1 tablespoon light brown sugar
1 dried red chili pepper, deseeded

1 Peel the chayote, holding it in a bowl of water (**photo A**). Quarter the chayote and remove the core. Cut each quarter into ½ in (1 cm) thick pieces.

2 Put the other ingredients in a saucepan and bring to a boil. Add the chayote and mix (**photo B**). Remove the pan from the heat. When cooled to room temperature, transfer the chayote to a bowl, leaving the liquid in the pan.

3 Bring the pan back to a boil. Put the chayote back into the pan and immediately remove the pan from the heat. When cooled, transfer the contents of the pan to the storage jar.

Spicy Chayote Pickles

From left to right: Thyme-scented Zucchni Pickles,
Curried Cauliflower Pickles and Piquant Cucumber Pickles

Thyme Scented Zucchini Pickles

The fragrance of thyme and the bright colors of this zucchini pickle delight the senses.

YIELDS: 8 oz (225 g)
PREPARATION TIME: 25 minutes

1 green zucchini, about 8 oz (225 g)
1 yellow zucchini, about 8 oz (225 g)

Pickling Solution
¾ cup (180 ml) rice vinegar
¾ cup (180 ml) water
⅔ cup (80 g) sugar
2 teaspoons salt
2 sprigs fresh thyme
1 bay leaf
1 dried red chili pepper, deseeded

CONTAINER ▸ 1 quart (1 liter) airtight storage jar
AGING ▸ 3 days in a cool, dark place
STORAGE ▸ Keeps 1 month in the refrigerator

1 Cut the zucchini into rounds ¼ in (5 mm) thick.

2 Have on hand a colander in the sink. Fill a large saucepan with water and bring to a boil. Add the zucchini rounds. When the water comes to a boil again, blanch the zucchini for 30 seconds and then drain into the colander.

3 Put the pickling solution ingredients into a separate saucepan. Bring to a boil over medium heat, remove from the heat and let cool.

4 Put the zucchini rounds in the storage jar (**photo A**). Pour in the pickling solution (**photo B**). Close the jar and put it in a cool, dark place for 3 days.

Curried Cauliflower Pickles

These tasty pickles are crunchy when first made, but soften and become more flavorful as they age.

YIELDS: 8 oz (225 g)
PREPARATION TIME: 30 minutes

1 head cauliflower, about 1 lb (450 g)
Water for boiling

Pickling Solution
1¼ cups (300 ml) rice vinegar
¾ cup (180 ml) water
⅔ cup (80 g) sugar
1 tablespoon kosher or coarse sea salt
2 teaspoons curry powder
1 teaspoon cumin seeds
1 bay leaf
1 dried red chili pepper, deseeded

CONTAINER ▶ 1 quart (1 liter) airtight storage jar
AGING ▶ 3 days in a cool, dark place
STORAGE ▶ Keeps 1 month in the refrigerator

1 Break the cauliflower into individual florets.

2 Have on hand a colander in the sink. Bring a large saucepan of water to a boil. Add the cauliflower. When the water comes to a boil again, blanch for 30 seconds (**photo A**) and then drain into the colander.

3 Put the pickling solution ingredients into a saucepan. On medium heat, bring to a boil and then remove from the heat.

4 Put the cauliflower pieces in the jar. Pour in the pickling solution (**photo B**). Seal and store in a cool, dark place for 3 days.

Piquant Cucumber Pickles

Parboiling prior to pickling helps to preserve flavor and extend shelf life. All the recipes in this book use Japanese cucumbers, which are slender with thin skin. You can also use Persian or mini cucumbers.

YIELDS: 10 oz (280 g)
PREPARATION TIME: 30 minutes

1 lb (450 g) cucumbers
1 teaspoon kosher or coarse sea salt
1 garlic clove

Pickling Solution
1¼ cups (300 ml) rice vinegar

⅔ cup (150 ml) water
4 tablespoons sugar
2 teaspoons kosher or coarse sea salt
1 bay leaf
½ teaspoon black peppercorns

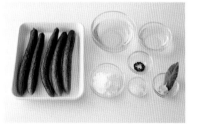

1 Cut off both ends of the cucumbers and then cut the cucumbers in half. Rub the 1 teaspoon of salt into them. This will help to preserve their color and reduce unwanted microorganisms.

2 Have on hand a colander in the sink. Fill a large saucepan with water and bring to a boil. Add the cucumbers and blanch for 30 seconds. Drain in the colander.

3 Put the pickling solution ingredients into a saucepan. On medium heat, bring to a boil and then remove from the heat.

4 Place the garlic into the airtight jar. Pack the cucumbers so that they will all be entirely covered by the pickling solution. Pour in the pickling solution. Close the jar and put it in a cool, dark place for 3 days.

CONTAINER ▶ 1 quart (1 liter) airtight storage jar
AGING ▶ 3 days in a cool, dark place
STORAGE ▶ Keeps 2 months in the refrigerator

Brined Melons

The recipes on this page are made with Oriental pickling melons (the long, not round, type), which are common in Japan, where they are called *shiro uri*. You may find these nonsweet melons at your Asian market in August or September. If you can't get hold of them, try using Kirby cucumbers (small, crisp cucumbers that are great for pickling), regular cucumber, chayote, or green papaya.

YIELDS: 8 oz (225 g)
PREPARATION TIME: 30 minutes

2 cups (500 ml) water
1½ tablespoons kosher or coarse sea salt
2 Oriental pickling melons (long, not round), totaling 1 lb (450 g)
6 green shiso leaves
2 green jalapeno peppers

CONTAINER ▸ 1 quart (1 liter) resealable storage bag
AGING ▸ 12 hours in the refrigerator
STORAGE ▸ Keeps 1 week in the refrigerator

 **1** Bring the 2 cups of water to boil in a saucepan. Add the salt and dissolve it completely. Remove the pan from the heat. This is the brine that you will use in step 4.

 **2** Fresh oriental pickling melons have tiny hairs that can irritate the skin. Wash the melons by rubbing them with your hands. Partially peel the melons, leaving strips of skin still on (see facing page, bottom photo).

3 Trim off both ends of the melons and then halve the melons. Use a spoon to scoop out the seeds.

 **4** Cut the shiso leaves into thin strips. Cut the chili peppers in half diagonally. Put the melons and the brine from step 1 into the storage bag. Add the shiso and chili peppers. Leave the bag in the refrigerator for at least 12 hours. Slice to serve.

Melons Pickled in Soy Sauce

Shredded dried kombu gives great umami.

YIELDS: 8 oz (225 g)
PREPARATION TIME: 20 minutes

2 Oriental pickling melons (long, not round), totaling about 1 lb (450 g)
4 tablespoons light soy sauce
3 tablespoons rice vinegar
1 teaspoon sugar
Handful julienned dried kombu seaweed
1 dried red chili pepper

CONTAINER ▸ 1 quart (1 liter) resealable storage bag
AGING ▸ 1 hour in a cool, dark place
STORAGE ▸ Keeps 1 week in the refrigerator

 **1** Halve the melon and cut into ½ in (1 cm) slices.

2 Put the soy sauce, vinegar and sugar into the storage bag and mix well. Add the melon, kombu and chili. Gently massage the bag. Expel the air from the bag, seal and refrigerate for 1 hour.

Melons Pickled in Miso

These crunchy, flavorful pickles are quick to make.

YIELDS: 8 pieces
PREPARATION TIME: 20 minutes

4 Oriental pickling melons (round, not long), totaling about 1 lb (450 g)
6 tablespoons miso
1 tablespoon mirin

EQUIPMENT ▸ Metal tray; plastic wrap
AGING ▸ 12 hours in the refrigerator
STORAGE ▸ Keeps 1 week in the refrigerator

 **1** Rub the melons in a bowl of water to remove hairs on the skin. Halve the melons and remove the seeds.

2 In a bowl mix the miso and mirin well. Fill the melon halves with this mixture.

3 Put the melon halves into the metal tray. Place a sheet of plastic wrap on top. Refrigerate for 12 hours. Slice to serve.

Melons Pickled in Soy Sauce

Melons Pickled in Miso

Brined Melons

Pickled Mini Eggplants

Small, soft-skinned eggplants are traditional favorites for pickling in Japan. Try Italian or Indian mini eggplant varieties in this recipe.

YIELDS: 16 mini eggplants
PREPARATION TIME: 15 minutes

16 mini eggplants, about 1 lb (450 g)
1 teaspoon alum, optional
1 tablespoon kosher or coarse sea salt
1 tablespoon sugar
4–5 green shiso leaves
¾ cup (180 ml) water

EQUIPMENT ▶ Metal tray; plastic gloves; 1 quart (1 liter) resealable storage bag; weights totaling 2 lb (1 kg)
AGING ▶ 1 day in the refrigerator
STORAGE ▶ Keeps 1–2 weeks in the refrigerator

1 Remove the stems from the eggplants, and put the eggplants into the metal tray. If using alum, put on the gloves and rub the alum onto the eggplants.

2 Sprinkle the salt and sugar onto the eggplants and then roll the eggplants around in the tray to make sure they are evenly coated.

3 Continue rolling the eggplants around until you see a purple liquid accumulating in the tray.

4 Put the eggplants and shiso leaves in the storage bag. Pour the ¾ cup of water into the metal tray and then pour all of the liquid in the tray into the storage bag.

5 Put the weight on top of the eggplants and then put the metal tray into the refrigerator for 1 day.

SERVING SUGGESTION
Pickle Sushi

Make a dressing of 3 parts rice vinegar and 1 part sugar and add to cooked short grain white rice to make sushi rice. Form the sushi rice into bite-size oblong shapes. Top each of these with a Salted Mini Eggplant or Sweetened Myoga Pickle. Put a tiny dollop of mustard on top of the eggplant and a few sesame seeds on the myoga.

Eggplant Pickled in Sweet Sake Lees and Mustard

If you can't get hold of mini Japanese eggplants, Italian or Indian mini varieties will work well.

YIELDS: 18 mini eggplants
PREPARATION TIME: 45 minutes plus 3 hours

18–20 mini eggplants, about 1 lb (450 g)
1 teaspoon alum, optional
1 tablespoon kosher or coarse sea salt
1 tablespoon sugar
1¼ cups (300 ml) water

Pickling Bed
¾ cup (225 g) sake lees paste
⅔ cup (80 g) sugar
2 tablespoons mustard powder
1 tablespoon kosher or coarse sea salt

EQUIPMENT ▸ Metal tray; plastic gloves; 1 quart (1 liter) resealable storage bag; 1½ quart (1.5 liter) storage container; plastic wrap
AGING ▸ 1 day in the refrigerator
STORAGE ▸ Keeps 2 weeks in the refrigerator

1 Follow steps 1–3 on the facing page to prepare the eggplants.

2 When a purple liquid accumulates in the tray, transfer the eggplants to the storage bag. Pour the 1¼ cups of water into the tray and then pour all the liquid in the tray into the storage bag (**photo A**). Refrigerate for about 3 hours.

3 Put the pickling bed ingredients in a bowl and mix well (**photo B**). If difficult to mix, transfer the ingredients to a plastic bag and massage the bag.

4 Put half of the pickling bed mixture into the storage container to create the bottom layer of the bed. Wipe each of the eggplants dry and place them on top of the bed, in lines and rows. Add the remaining pickling bed mixture, pushing it down in between the eggplants and leveling off the top as much as possible (**photos C and D**).

5 Put a sheet of plastic wrap directly on top of the eggplants and pickling bed mixture. The sheet should be big enough to run up the sides of the container. Refrigerate for 1 day.

EGGPLANTS
Japanese eggplants are small, slender and soft-skinned and are a favorite pickling ingredient. If you can't find Japanese eggplants, Chinese eggplants (long and thin with a light color) are similar. For recipes that use Japanese mini eggplants, try Italian or Indian varieties.

Mini Eggplant Jar Pickles

Mini eggplant pickles are wonderfully juicy. Look for Italian and Indian varieties.

YIELDS: 18–20 eggplants
PREPARATION TIME: 50 minutes

⅔ cup (80 g) sugar
3 tablespoons kosher or coarse sea salt
2 teaspoons alum, optional
2 cups (500 ml) water
18–20 mini eggplants, about 1 lb (450 g)
2–3 green shiso leaves

CONTAINER ▸ 1 quart (1 liter) airtight storage jar
AGING ▸ 1 day in the refrigerator
STORAGE ▸ Keeps 2 weeks in the refrigerator

1 Put the sugar, salt, alum (if using) and water in a saucepan, bring to a boil and then remove from the heat.

2 Trim the eggplants. Soak in water for 30 minutes, then drain.

3 Pack the eggplants into the storage jar as tightly as possible. Pour in the cooled contents of the pan and place the shiso leaves on top of the eggplants (see photo). Put the jar into the refrigerator for 1 day.

Eggplant in Soy Sauce

Key here is to let the eggplant rest for 30 minutes after salting, then removing excess water to let flavor in.

YIELDS: 4 oz (115 g)
PREPARATION TIME: 50 minutes

6 oz (170 g) slender Asian eggplant
½ teaspoon kosher or coarse sea salt
2 teaspoons soy sauce
1 teaspoon grated fresh ginger
1 teaspoon roasted white sesame seeds

CONTAINER ▸ 1 quart (1 liter) resealable storage bag
AGING ▸ 30 minutes in the refrigerator
STORAGE ▸ Keeps 3 days in the refrigerator

1 Trim the eggplant, halve lengthways and then slice each half thinly. Soak in water for about 5 minutes, then drain.

2 Put the eggplant pieces into the storage bag. Add the salt, seal and shake to coat the pieces evenly. Leave in a cool, dark place for 30 minutes.

3 Open the bag and squeeze excess water from the eggplant. Return the eggplant to the bag and add the rest of the ingredients. After massaging the bag to mix, the pickle is ready for eating.

Mizu-Nasu Eggplant Pickles

Mizu-nasu literally means "water eggplant," a Japanese variety that is so sweet and tender it can be eaten raw. Outside of Japan you may be able to find it at farmers' markets, or you could try growing your own from seed.

YIELDS: 1 eggplant
PREPARATION TIME: 15 minutes

1 mizu-nasu eggplant
1 piece dried kombu seaweed, 2 in (5 cm) square
½ teaspoon alum, optional
½ teaspoon sugar
½ teaspoon rice vinegar
½ teaspoon mirin
⅔ teaspoon kosher or coarse sea salt
½ cup (125 ml) water

CONTAINER ▸ 1 quart (1 liter) resealable storage bag
AGING ▸ 1 day in the refrigerator
STORAGE ▸ Keeps 5 days in the refrigerator

1 Put the eggplant and the kombu to one side. Place all the other ingredients in a saucepan and bring to a boil. Remove from the heat and let cool.

2 Remove the stems and petals from the top of the eggplant.

3 Put the eggplant into the storage bag, add the kombu and then pour in the cooled contents of the pan. Expel the air from the bag. Seal the bag and put it into the refrigerator for 1 day.

4 To eat, divide the pickled eggplant into smaller pieces by making cuts in the bottom and pulling it apart.

Shio Koji Pickled Eggplant

Shio-koji rice-malt seasoning adds great umami and depth of flavor to tender mizu-nasu eggplant.

YIELDS: 1 eggplant
PREPARATION TIME: 15 minutes

1 mizu-nasu eggplant
1 tablespoon shio koji paste
Handful julienned dried kombu seaweed

CONTAINER ▶ 1 quart (1 liter) resealable storage bag
AGING ▶ 1 hour in a cool, dark place
STORAGE ▶ Keeps 3 days in the refrigerator

1 Remove the stems and petals from the top of the eggplant. Halve the eggplant and then cut it into diagonal slices about ½ in (1 cm) thick.

2 Put the eggplant slices into the storage bag. Add the shio koji and kombu and mix.

3 Expel the air from the bag. Seal the bag and put it into the refrigerator for 1 hour.

Sweet Myoga Pickles

Myoga is a fresh Japanese ginger bulb with a light flavor and aroma. You may spot it at Japanese groceries. Grab it when you see it!

YIELDS: 10 pieces
PREPARATION TIME: 25 minutes

10 myoga ginger buds
⅓ cup (75 ml) rice vinegar
2 tablespoons water
3 tablespoons sugar
1 teaspoon kosher or coarse sea salt

CONTAINER ▶ 1 pint (500 ml) storage container
AGING ▶ 12 hours in the refrigerator
STORAGE ▶ Keeps 1–2 weeks in the refrigerator

1 Cut each myoga bud in half, lengthways.

2 Bring a medium saucepan of water to a boil. Add the myoga. When the water comes back to a boil, wait 10 seconds and then remove the myoga with a sieve.

3 Put all the other ingredients in a separate saucepan (**photo A**). Bring to a boil, remove from the heat and allow to cool.

4 Put the myoga in the storage container and pour in the contents of the pan (**photo B**). Refrigerate for 12 hours.

Vinegar Pickled Myoga

Myoga keeps well in the refrigerator but is best eaten soon after making when its texture is firm.

YIELD: 10 pieces
PREPARATION TIME: 20 minutes

10 myoga ginger buds
½ cup (125 ml) water
3 tablespoons rice vinegar
1 tablespoon sugar
1 tablespoon light soy sauce
⅓ cup (4 g) dried bonito flakes

CONTAINER ▶ 1 pint (500 ml) storage container
AGING ▶ 12 hours in the refrigerator
STORAGE ▶ Keeps 1 month in the refrigerator

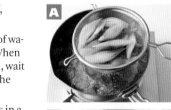

1 Cut each myoga bud in half, lengthways. Bring a saucepan of water to a boil. Add the myoga. When the water comes back to a boil, wait 10 seconds and remove the myoga with a sieve (**photo A**).

2 Put the water, vinegar, sugar and soy sauce in a separate saucepan. Bring to a boil, then remove from the heat. Add the bonito and let cool.

3 Put the myoga in the storage container and pour in the contents of the pan (**photo B**). Refrigerate for 12 hours.

Cherry Tomatoes in Honey and Balsamic Vinegar

The concentrated flavor of balsamic vinegar accentuates the sweet-sour taste of cherry tomatoes.

YIELDS: 8 oz (225 g)
PREPARATION TIME: 30 minutes

20 cherry tomatoes, about 10 oz (280 g)
2 tablespoons balsamic vinegar
1 tablespoon water
1 tablespoon honey
½ teaspoon kosher or coarse sea salt

CONTAINER ▸ 1½ quart (1.5 liter) storage container
AGING ▸ 12 hours in the refrigerator
STORAGE ▸ Keeps 1 week in the refrigerator

1 Remove the stems from the cherry tomatoes.

2 Bring a saucepan of water to a boil. Add the tomatoes. When their skins split, transfer them to a bowl of cold water and peel.

3 Put all the other ingredients in the storage container and mix well. Add the tomatoes. Refrigerate for 12 hours. Jostle the container periodically during this time.

Sweet Sake Pickles

This recipe works well for any non-leafy vegetable.

YIELDS: 6 oz (170 g)
PREPARATION TIME: 35 minutes

½ carrot
½ red bell pepper
½ yellow bell pepper
1 stalk celery
1 Japanese cucumber
½ cup (125 ml) Amazake Mash (see page 86)
3 tablespoons rice vinegar
1½ teaspoons kosher or coarse sea salt
1 garlic clove, crushed
1 bay leaf

CONTAINER ▸ 1½ quart (1.5 liter) storage container
AGING ▸ 1 day in the refrigerator
STORAGE ▸ Keeps 1 week in the refrigerator

1 Cut the vegetables into ½ in x 2 in (1 cm x 5 cm) batons.

2 Put all the other ingredients in a bowl and mix well.

3 Add the vegetables to the bowl and stir to coat with the pickling solution. Transfer the contents of the bowl to the storage container. Refrigerate for 1 day.

Bitter Melon with Plum

Bitter melon is known as *goya* in Japan, where it is a popular vegetable. Find it at Asian markets.

YIELDS: 4 oz (115 g)
PREPARATION TIME: 25 minutes

1 bitter melon, about 8 oz (225 g)
1 umeboshi pickled plum, soft type, pit removed
⅓ cup (4 g) dried bonito flakes
2 teaspoons light brown sugar

CONTAINER ▸ 1 quart (1 liter) resealable storage bag
AGING ▸ 30 minutes in the refrigerator
STORAGE ▸ Keeps 3 days in the refrigerator

1 Halve the bitter melon and use a spoon to scrape out the seeds and fibres. Cut the halves into ¼ in (5 mm) slices. Chop the flesh of the umeboshi into a paste.

2 Bring a medium saucepan of water to a boil. Add the bitter melon slices. When the water comes back to a boil, remove the melon and put in a bowl of cold water.

3 Put the bitter melon, umeboshi and bonito in a bag and mix. Refrigerate for 30 minutes.

Sweet & Sour Bitter Melon

Bitterness and salty sweetness come together for a flavor sensation you'll crave time and again.

YIELDS: 4 oz (115 g)
PREPARATION TIME: 20 minutes

1 bitter melon, about 8 oz (225 g)
Small piece fresh ginger, julienned

Pickling Solution
4 tablespoons light soy sauce
4 tablespoons rice vinegar
2 tablespoons light brown sugar
1 dried red chili pepper, deseeded

CONTAINER ▸ 1½ quart (1.5 liter) airtight storage jar
AGING ▸ None
STORAGE ▸ Keeps 1 week in the refrigerator

1 Halve the bitter melon and use a spoon to scrape out the seeds and fibres. Cut the halves into ½ in x 2 in (1 cm x 5 cm) lengths.

2 Put the pickling solution ingredients in a saucepan over medium heat. When the pan comes to a boil, add the melon slices and ginger. When the pan comes back to a boil, remove from the heat and let cool. Transfer the contents of the pan to the airtight jar.

Shiso Leaves Marinated in Garlic Soy Sauce

Roll a leaf of pickled shiso around a bit of rice, pop it into your mouth and experience simple, yet exquisite pleasure. Serve with a dash of Korean red chili pepper for a hint of kimchi goodness.

YIELDS: 30 leaves
PREPARATION TIME: 20 minutes

30 green shiso leaves
2 garlic cloves
4 tablespoons soy sauce
1 tablespoon sesame oil

EQUIPMENT ▸ 1 pint (500 ml) storage container; plastic wrap
AGING ▸ 12 hours in the refrigerator
STORAGE ▸ Keeps 1 month in the refrigerator

1 Hold the shiso leaves all together by the stems and rinse them in a bowl of water.

2 Spread the leaves out and use a paper towel to pat them dry. Remove the cores and any green sprouts from the garlic cloves and then slice thinly.

3 Lay the shiso leaves flat in the storage container. Sprinkle on the garlic slices. Pour in the soy sauce and then add the sesame oil.

4 Place a piece of plastic wrap directly on top of the shiso leaves. Refrigerate for 12 hours.

Soy Cured Shiso Seeds

These pickled seeds are marvelous as a topping for rice and tofu and as an ingredient for sushi rice.

YIELDS: 4 oz (115 g)
PREPARATION TIME: 45 minutes

4 oz (115 g) green shiso seeds (see note, below)
½ cup (125 ml) soy sauce
4 tablespoons mirin
1 teaspoon grated ginger
*4 oz is the yield of 4½ oz (130 g) of shiso seed heads

EQUIPMENT ▸ Plastic gloves; 1 pint (500 ml) storage jar
AGING ▸ 2 days in the refrigerator
STORAGE ▸ Keeps 6 months in the refrigerator

Salted Shiso Seeds

Shiso seeds, also known as perilla seeds, are high in omega-3 fatty acids, essential for good health. This recipe uses the young green seeds, which you can find at your Asian market.

YIELDS: 4 oz (115 g)
PREPARATION TIME: 35 minutes

4 oz (115 g) green shiso seeds (see note, below)
1½ tablespoons kosher or coarse sea salt
*4 oz is the yield of 4½ oz (130 g) of shiso seed heads

EQUIPMENT ▸ Plastic gloves; 1 pint (500 ml) storage jar
AGING ▸ 2 days in the refrigerator
STORAGE ▸ Keeps 1 year in the refrigerator

1 Hold the shiso seed heads upside down and strip off the seeds. Wear plastic gloves if you have sensitive skin.

2 Soak the seeds in a bowl of water. Stir them around to release any dirt. When thoroughly cleaned, drain them in a sieve.

3 Put the soy sauce and mirin in a small saucepan. Bring to a boil then remove from the heat. Let cool, then add the ginger.

4 Bring a pan of water to a boil. Put in the seeds. When the water comes back to a boil, remove the seeds and transfer to a bowl of cold water. This eliminates unwanted flavors and retains the color. Drain in a sieve, squeezing out excess water.

5 Put the seeds into the storage jar and add the soy sauce, mirin and ginger mixture. Stir the jar well and refrigerate for 2 days.

1 Follow steps 1, 2 and 4 for Soy Cured Shiso Seeds (this page).
2 Put the seeds into the storage jar and add the salt. Stir the jar well and then leave in the refrigerator for 2 days.

GREEN SHISO SEEDS
In Japan, fresh green shiso seeds, sold as seed heads, become available in the latter half of summer. The seeds develop after the shiso plant has produced the flowers used to garnish sashimi. Shiso seeds harden as they age, so knowledgeable consumers look for young seed heads with seeds that are still soft.

Salted Shiso Seeds

Soy Cured Shiso Seeds

Sweet Lotus Root Pickles

This pickle is delicious when mixed into sushi rice or as a side dish with fish.

YIELDS: 8 oz (225 g)
PREPARATION TIME: 30 minutes

1 piece lotus root, about 8 oz (225 g)
1 piece dried kombu seaweed, 2 in (5 cm) square
1 dried red chili pepper

Pickling Solution
½ cup (125 ml) rice vinegar
4 tablespoons water
3 tablespoons sugar
2 tablespoons mirin
1 teaspoon kosher or coarse sea salt

CONTAINER ▸ 1 pint (500 ml) storage jar
AGING ▸ 12 hours in the refrigerator
STORAGE ▸ Keeps 1 month in the refrigerator

1 Peel the lotus root and slice into thin rounds (**photo A**). Rinse in water and drain.

2 Bring a medium saucepan of water to a boil. Put in the lotus root. When the water returns to a boil, wait for 1 minute, then remove the lotus root with a sieve (**photo B**).

3 Put the pickling solution ingredients in a separate pan. Bring to a boil, remove from the heat and let cool.

4 Put the lotus root slices into the storage jar, and add the kombu, red chili pepper and pickling solution. Refrigerate for 1 hour.

Spicy Lotus Root Pickles

Chili oil and sesame oil give a Chinese flavor to this pickle.

YIELDS: 6 oz (170 g)
PREPARATION TIME: 30 minutes

1 piece lotus root, about 8 oz (225 g)
2 tablespoons rice vinegar
1 tablespoon sugar
2 teaspoons soy sauce
⅓ teaspoon kosher or coarse sea salt
1 teaspoon chili oil
2 teaspoons sesame oil
1 dried red chili pepper, sliced into rings

CONTAINER ▸ 1 quart (1 liter) resealable storage bag
AGING ▸ 12 hours in the refrigerator
STORAGE ▸ Keeps 1 month in the refrigerator

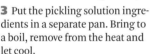

1 Peel the lotus root and cut into thin batons (**photo**). Rinse in water.

2 Bring a medium saucepan of water to a boil. Put in the lotus root. When the water returns to a boil, wait for 1 minute, then remove the lotus root with a sieve.

3 Put all the other ingredients into the storage bag and mix. Add the lotus root. Refrigerate for 12 hours.

Mustard Pickled Lotus Root

A touch of mustard adds depth to this sweet-and-sour pickle.

YIELDS: 6 oz (170 g)
PREPARATION TIME: 30 minutes

1 piece lotus root, about 8 oz (225 g)
2 tablespoons wholegrain mustard
1½ tablespoons soy sauce
2 tablespoons rice vinegar
½ tablespoon honey

CONTAINER ▸ 1 quart (1 liter) resealable storage bag
AGING ▸ 12 hours in the refrigerator
STORAGE ▸ Keeps 1–2 weeks in the refrigerator

1 Peel the lotus root and slice into thin rounds. Rinse in water and drain.

2 Bring a medium saucepan of water to a boil. Put in the lotus root. When the water returns to a boil, wait for 1 minute, then remove the lotus root with a sieve.

3 Put the rest of the ingredients into the storage bag and mix. Add the lotus root and massage the bag. Refrigerate for 12 hours.

Sweet Lotus Root Pickles

Spicy Lotus Root Pickles

Mustard Pickled Lotus Root

Crunchy Korinki Squash Pickles

Cut these pickles into large pieces to enjoy their crispy texture. Mince them to add color to salads.

YIELDS: 6 oz (170 g)
PREPARATION TIME: 25 minutes

½ Korinki squash, about 12 oz (350g), (see note, facing page)
1 piece dried kombu seaweed, 2 in (5 cm) square
1 dried red chili pepper, deseeded

Pickling Solution
1 tablespoon light soy sauce
1 tablespoon mirin
1 tablespoon light brown sugar
½ teaspoon kosher or coarse sea salt
2 tablespoons rice vinegar
½ cup (125 ml) water

CONTAINER ▶ 1 quart (1 liter) resealable storage bag
AGING ▶ 12 hours in the refrigerator
STORAGE ▶ Keeps 2 weeks in the refrigerator

1 Halve the korinki squash and use a spoon to remove the seeds and fibres.

2 Peel the squash and cut into ¼ in (5 mm) wedges.

3 Put the pickling solution ingredients in a saucepan. Bring to a boil, remove from the heat and let cool.

4 Put the squash into the storage bag. Add the kombu and red chili pepper, and then pour in the cooled contents of the pan. Put the storage bag into the refrigerator for 12 hours.

Korinki Squash and Cucumber with Shio Kombu

Vibrant orange squash combined with green shio kombu salted kelp will perk up your dinner table.

YIELDS: 8 oz (225 g)
PREPARATION TIME: 25 minutes

¼ Korinki squash, about 6 oz (170g), (see note below)
1 Japanese cucumber
½ oz (15 g) shio kombu salted kelp

CONTAINER ▸ 1 quart (1 liter) resealable storage bag
AGING ▸ 1 hour in a cool, dark place
STORAGE ▸ Keeps 5 days in the refrigerator

A

B

1 Halve the korinki squash and use a spoon to remove the seeds and fibres. Slice thinly, leaving the skin on. Cut the cucumber into ¼ in (5 mm) rounds.

2 Put the squash and cucumbers into the storage bag, add the shio kombu and massage the bag (**photo A**).

3 Expel the air from the bag. Seal the bag and put it into the refrigerator for 1 hour (**photo B**).

NOTE: If you're really in a hurry you can reduce the time of pickling process by massaging the bag for longer and leaving for 30 minutes at room temperature.

KORINKI SQUASH
Korinki are unique among squashes as they can be eaten raw. Their crunchy texture makes for a great pickle. If you can't find korinki squash, green papaya is a good substitute.

Mediterranean Mushrooms

The sweet and concentrated flavor of balsamic vinegar goes magnificently with mushrooms. Try these on bread or with pasta.

YIELDS: 8 oz (225 g)
PREPARATION TIME: 30 minutes

1 lb (450 g) mixed mushrooms (button, shimeji, eringi, or any others)
1 garlic clove
2 tablespoons olive oil, for frying
1 teaspoon kosher or coarse sea salt
4 tablespoons balsamic vinegar
1 dried red chili pepper, deseeded
1 bay leaf
½ cup (125 ml) olive oil

CONTAINER ▸ 1 pint (500 ml) airtight storage jar
AGING ▸ 1 day in a cool, dark place
STORAGE ▸ Keeps 2 weeks in the refrigerator

1 Cut off the tough ends of the mushroom stems. Quarter the button mushrooms and eringi, and break the shimeji into smaller pieces. Crush the garlic clove.

2 Put the 2 tablespoons of olive oil and the garlic in a frying pan over low heat. When the garlic starts to become fragrant, add the mushrooms and turn the heat to medium (**photo A**).

3 When the mushrooms have softened, sprinkle with the salt and add the vinegar, chili and bay leaf. Continue cooking for 3–4 minutes, until most of the liquid has disappeared (**photo B**). Remove the pan from the heat.

4 After the mushrooms have cooled, transfer to the storage jar and add the ½ cup of olive oil (**photo C**). Leave in a cool, dark place for 1 day.

Mushrooms in Soy Sauce

With a sesame aroma to stoke the appetite, these mixed mushrooms are an ideal match for rice, tofu and noodle dishes.

YIELDS: 8 oz (225 g)
PREPARATION TIME: 30 minutes

1 lb (450 g) mixed mushrooms (fresh shiitake, enoki, shimeji, eringi, or any others)
1 tablespoon soy sauce
1 tablespoon mirin
1 teaspoon rice vinegar
½ teaspoon kosher or coarse sea salt
1 dried red chili pepper, deseeded
1 teaspoon sesame oil

CONTAINER ▸ 1 pint (500 ml) storage container
AGING ▸ 1–2 hours in a cool, dark place
STORAGE ▸ Keeps 2 weeks in the refrigerator.

1 Cut off the tough ends of the mushroom stems. Split the shiitake into quarters (stems and caps together), break the shimeji into smaller pieces, quarter the eringi and separate the enoki into small bundles.

2 Bring a medium saucepan of water to a boil. Put in the mushrooms. When the water returns to a boil, wait for 1 minute, then remove the mushrooms with a sieve.

3 When the mushrooms have cooled, transfer them to the storage container. Mix all the other ingredients together and pour over the mushrooms. Leave in a cool, dark place for 1–2 hours.

Mushrooms in Soy Sauce

Mediterranean Mushrooms

Daikon and Carrot Pickles

Here I've used red Kyoto carrot, but regular orange carrot is fine.

YIELDS: 10 oz (280 g)
PREPARATION TIME: 35 minutes plus 1 hour

½ daikon radish, about 1lb (450 g)
1 large carrot, about 4 oz (115 g)
1 teaspoon kosher or coarse sea salt
5 tablespoons sugar
2 teaspoons kosher or coarse sea salt
2 tablespoons rice vinegar
Zest of 1 yuzu citrus, julienned
2 tablespoons yuzu juice

CONTAINER ▸ 1 quart (1 liter) resealable storage bag
AGING ▸ 2 hours in a cool, dark place
STORAGE ▸ Keeps 2 weeks in the refrigerator

1 Peel and julienne the daikon and carrot. Cut the daikon a little bit thicker than the carrot.

2 Put the daikon and carrot into a bowl and add the salt. Leave in a cool, dark place for 1 hour.

3 After an hour, squeeze the water out of the daikon and carrot and transfer to the storage bag. Add the rest of the ingredients. Massage the bag to mix (**see photo**). Leave in a cool, dark place for 1 hour.

Miso Cured Daikon

These pickles are ready when the daikon chunks soften and lose their sharp edges.

YIELDS: 10 oz (280 g)
PREPARATION TIME: 25 minutes plus 1 hour

½ daikon radish, about 1 lb (450 g)
2 teaspoons kosher or coarse sea salt (2% of the weight of the daikon)
2 tablespoons sugar (4% of the weight of the daikon)
3½ tablespoons miso (10% of the weight of the daikon)

EQUIPMENT ▸ 1 quart (1 liter) resealable storage bag; metal tray; weights totaling 1¼ lbs (600 g)
AGING ▸ 4 hours in the refrigerator
STORAGE ▸ Keeps 1 week in the refrigerator

1 Peel the daikon and cut into 1 in x 2 in (2.5 cm x 5 cm) lengths.

2 Put the daikon into the storage bag and add the salt and sugar. Expel the air from the bag and seal. Put the bag into a tray and put the weight on top of the bag. Refrigerate for 1 hour.

3 Open the bag and drain off the water that has accumulated. Add the miso. Seal the bag and massage it to mix the contents (**see photo**). Refrigerate for 3 hours.

Citrus Daikon Pickles

If you can't get hold of Japanese yuzu citrus, use lemon instead.

YIELDS: 10 oz (280 g)
PREPARATION TIME: 30 minutes

½ daikon radish, about 1 lb (450 g)
1 tablespoon kosher or coarse sea salt (3% of the weight of the daikon)
4 tablespoons sugar
Pinch kosher or coarse sea salt
1 tablespoon rice vinegar
Zest of 1 yuzu citrus, julienned
1 tablespoon yuzu juice

EQUIPMENT ▸ 1 quart (1 liter) resealable storage bag; metal tray; weights totaling 2 lb (1 kg)
AGING ▸ 1 day in a cool, dark place
STORAGE ▸ Keeps 1 week in the refrigerator

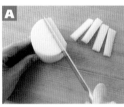

1 Peel the daikon and cut into ¼ in x 2 in (5 mm x 5 cm) batons (**photo A**).

2 Put the daikon into the storage bag and add the salt. Expel the air from the bag and seal. Put the bag into a tray and put the weight on top. Leave in a cool, dark place for 1 hour.

3 Open the bag and drain the water that has accumulated. Put in the rest of the ingredients. Massage the bag. Leave in a cool, dark place for 12 hours.

Beer Pickled Daikon

The yeast in beer aids fermentation, and mustard powder accentuates the flavor.

YIELDS: 10 oz (280 g)
PREPARATION TIME: 20 minutes plus 1 hour

½ daikon radish, about 1 lb (450 g)
2 teaspoons kosher or coarse sea salt
2 tablespoons beer
3 tablespoons light brown sugar
1 teaspoon kosher or coarse sea salt
1 teaspoon mustard powder
4 teaspoons rice vinegar

CONTAINER ▸ 1 quart (1 liter) resealable storage bag
AGING ▸ 1 day in a cool, dark place
STORAGE ▸ Keeps 1 week in the refrigerator

1 Peel and quarter the daikon. Cut each quarter into thin slices.

2 Put the daikon into the storage bag and add the salt. Leave in a cool, dark place for 1 hour.

3 Open the bag and drain off the water that has accumulated. Add all the other ingredients and gently massage the bag. Leave in a cool, dark place for 12 hours.

Sauerkraut

Sauerkraut is a popular winter pickle. Simply salt chopped cabbage and wait for the lactic acid fermentation to do its job. Sourness intensifies as the fermentation continues, so taste your sauerkraut as it's fermenting and transfer to the refrigerator when it's as sour as you want it.

Caraway Studded Sauerkraut

A slowly sinking weight and rising bubbles will tell you the cabbage is properly fermenting. This sauerkraut is crunchier than traditional German sauerkraut.

YIELDS: 2 cups (300 g)
PREPARATION TIME: 35 minutes

½ head green or red cabbage, about 1 lb (450 g)
2 teaspoons kosher or coarse sea salt (2.5% of the weight of the cabbage)
1 bay leaf
½ tablespoon caraway seeds
⅔ cup (150 ml) water

EQUIPMENT ▸ 1½ quart (1.5 liter) airtight storage jar; 1 gallon (4 liter) plastic bag; jar that fits inside the storage jar for use as a weight
AGING ▸ 1 week at room temperature
STORAGE ▸ Keeps 1 month in the refrigerator

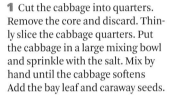

1 Cut the cabbage into quarters. Remove the core and discard. Thinly slice the cabbage quarters. Put the cabbage in a large mixing bowl and sprinkle with the salt. Mix by hand until the cabbage softens Add the bay leaf and caraway seeds.

2 Transfer the cabbage to the storage jar and add the water. Put a plastic bag bottom-first into the jar and push it down directly onto the cabbage. Drape the open end over and around the top edge of the jar.

3 Fill a smaller jar with water and seal (the total weight of this water-filled jar should be about 20% of the weight of the cabbage). Put this jar inside the bag, so it sits on the cabbage. Within the larger jar, the cabbage should all be in contact with the water. Close the larger jar by putting the storage lid over the plastic. You may need rubber bands to keep the lid in place.

4 In winter leave the jar at room temperature in a cool, dark place for 1 week. In warmer weather, leave for 3 days. Check frequently. Your sauerkraut will be ready when the cabbage turns yellow and you see bubbles in the liquid.

SERVING SUGGESTION
Sauerkraut Soup

Caraway Studded Sauerkraut is delicious in soup. Brown some onions, potatoes and bacon. Add sauerkraut and consommé, and simmer.

Napa Cabbage with Yuzu and Shio Koji

Yuzu citrus lends its wonderful fragrance to this Napa cabbage pickled in shio-koji rice-malt seasoning. If you can't find yuzu, use lemon.

YIELDS: 4 oz (115 g)
PREPARATION TIME: 25 minutes

8 oz (225 g) Napa cabbage
1 tablespoon shio koji paste
A little yuzu citrus zest, julienned, to taste
1 tablespoon yuzu juice

CONTAINER ▸ 1 quart (1 liter) resealable storage bag
AGING ▸ 30 minutes in a cool, dark place
STORAGE ▸ Keeps 2 weeks in the refrigerator

1 Cut the cabbage into ¼ in (5 mm) pieces.

2 Put the cabbage in the storage bag and add the other ingredients. Gently massage the bag. Leave in a cool, dark place for 30 minutes.

Hot and Sour Cabbage

Sesame oil and spicy peppers give this pickle a punch.

YIELDS: 12 oz (350 g)
PREPARATION TIME: 1 hour

¼ Napa cabbage core, about 12 oz (350 g)
½ teaspoon kosher or coarse sea salt
3 tablespoons rice vinegar
2 tablespoons light brown sugar
½ teaspoon kosher or coarse sea salt
2 tablespoons sesame oil
1 dried red chili pepper, sliced into rings
1 teaspoon Sichuan peppercorns

EQUIPMENT ▸ Heat-resistant mixing bowl
AGING ▸ 1 hour in a cool, dark place
STORAGE ▸ Keeps 1 week in the refrigerator

1 Cut the cabbage core into ¼ in x 2 in (5 mm x 5 cm) batons. Sprinkle with ½ teaspoon of salt and set aside. After 30 minutes, squeeze the excess water from the cabbage core.

2 Put the vinegar, sugar and the other ½ teaspoon of salt in a heat-resistant mixing bowl and mix. Mix in the cabbage-core pieces.

3 Put the sesame oil, chili and peppercorns in a frying pan over low heat. When the pan begins to smoke, pour the contents into the bowl containing the cabbage core. Leave in a cool, dark place for 30 minutes.